HIGH TIDE

the 2019 anthology
of poetry and prose

by members of

the Federation of Writers (Scotland)

Published 2019
by New Voices Press
imprint of the Federation of Writers (Scotland)

www.federationofwritersscotland.wordpress.com

ISBN 978-1-906708-21-4

Clip art courtesy of MariaFresa.net

Patrons

Dave Anderson, Carol Ann Duffy, Bashabi Fraser
Magi Gibson, Liz Lochhead, Christine de Luca
Carl MacDougall, Donny O'Rourke, Zoe Strachan
Rosemary Ward

	Makars	Scrievers
2008:	Robin Cairns	-
2009:	A C Clarke	-
2010:	Maggie Rabatski	-
2011:	Sheila Templeton	-
2012:	Colin Will	-
2013:	Rab Wilson	-
2014:	Anne Connolly	-
2015:	Brian Whittingham	-
2016:	Elizabeth Rimmer	-
2017:	Andy Jackson	-
2018:	Marjorie Lotfi Gill	-
2019:	Stephen Watt	Olga Wojtas

Introduction

High Tide reads as a celebration of Scotland — stories of old times, older folk, the old places, memories from and in the places that matter to us. The many beautiful pieces in Scots and Gaelic ground the collection, remind readers who is speaking and where they (and our words) come from.

I was particularly taken with the poems and stories looking back at a life (classroom antics, the death of a family member, accidents) and seeing it differently through the passage of time, hearing voices finally freed. They remind the reader to look again, ask different questions and reconsider what annoyed us, what let us down, how what actually happened might be different from what we remember. Others just tell the truth as it was, exploring the difficult in families, going back and revisiting the places and faces of youth.

The last clutch of poems in the collection focuses on water (a salt-wife, a fast river, the reef of dreams). These pieces remind us that we live on an island and that our lives are all touched by the water around us, whether that's as a beginning or renewing of life, and, as importantly, that these bodies of water will carry on despite us.

But mostly the pieces in *High Tide* ask us to look more closely, plucking out the ordinary and holding it up as something to behold, something extraordinary — a child's star brought down from the heavens in a public square, for example, or the art in a car garage. These poems and stories renew our belief in the magic of the everyday.

There are so many glittering stars to choose from in *High Tide*. It's a collection of work we'll all return to again and again.

Marjorie Lotfi Gill

Acknowledgements:

Anne Connolly *for anthology team leadership*
Janet Crawford *for co-ordinating the submissions process*
Charlie Gracie and **Catherine Hokin** *for prose selection*
Neil Leadbeater and **Sheila Templeton** *for English and Scots poetry selection*
Jenifer Harley *for production and distribution*
Loretta Serene Dunn *for cover design*
Marjorie Lotfi Gill *for her generous comments on* High Tide.

HIGH TIDE

Writers

	page
Andy Allan	8, 9
Morag Anderson	28
Fran Baillie	10
Emma Baker	34, 36, 38
Neil Beaton	26, 27
David Betteridge	15
Sharon Boyle	46, 52, 54
Derek Brown	18
Montague Chambers	104
A C Clarke	66, 67
Peter Clive	86
Derek Crook	44, 45
Seth Crook	16, 17
Meg Gannon	72, 73
Jo Gilbert	32, 33
Alan Gillespie	68
Tom Gillespie	29, 30
Colin Kerr	84
Jane Lamb	39
Ann MacKinnon	64, 65
Steve May	81, 102

	page
David McVey	23
Greg Michaelson	62
Sheila Millar	11
Deborah Moffatt	90
Mary Nixon	20
Paula Nicolson	57
Jilly O'Brien	92
Aileen Paterson	60, 61
Sue Proudlove	58, 59
Alun Robert	42
Hamish Scott	56
Swara Shukla	40
Leela Soma	74, 75, 76
William Sutton	95
Jean Taylor	77
Marie-Thérèse Taylor	25
Bert Thomson	82
Sgàire Uallas	88
Lynn Valentine	24
Elaine Webster	93
Mary Wight	94

HIGH TIDE

Andy Allan

Scots Pine

Your familiar rugged silhouette
looms through mist's damp gauze;
a grainy shadow, deep-rooted,
enduring the harsh grey years.
Buffeted by air and time,
heavy limbs flexing, swaying
as they have always done,
defiant, creaking,
sighing in the wind.
On high, your flaky skin's aflame,
splashed with flashing sunlit gold.
I smile as I finger-trace again,
those once familiar scars
gouged in your gnarled
deep-fissured trunk.
The faintest whispers seep
from memories of you.
Here hardy lichens cling
clad in fluttering green,
sifting wind-currents,
tiny anemones on a reef.

Andy Allan

An empty chair

Dust motes float in warm
still air filled with the scent
of fresh-cut flowers.
Bathed in filtered sunlight
neglected books lie piled
on a low table.
Disappointment leaches
from their silent leaves.
Some sprawl scattered
on carpet's dull wool pile,
their bright eye-trap covers
vying to snag attention.
Discarded,
one lies open, face down
beside a tattered bookmark.
Creeping time ticks
across a brass-faced clock
high on dated wallpaper.
Below,
the empty armchair waits.

Fran Baillie

Advice to a stripling

Sweet night has come at last, no sane soul's home.
Carpe noctem, sir. Gird those tender loins.
Open that purse, secrete some silver coins;
primp thy French lace ruff, preen thy bright cockscomb.
To a nightclub, methinks, we'll now repair
to strut, not fret, the hours upon the floor;
check out the bitches, that's what life is for
while we are blithe and young and free and fair.
Then let's quaff ale. Anon, let's quaff some more
and charm, and so seduce the gathered throng;
share jocund company, and then ere long
steer giddy, hand-plucked harlots through the door.
'Twas ever thus, greenhorn. You'll learn, my cove,
lads live to jag and brag and call this love.

Sheila Millar

The attic

Mabel Thresher left her attic room and locked the door behind her. The key rested with others in the chatelaine at her waist. From the little window she had watched the horizon draw down the sun, leaving wisps of cloud around the autumn moon. Now she hurried down to her garden hoping the dim light would be enough to let her tidy and trim, perhaps dead-head? The evening brought a misty crispness to her flower beds where the blooms were beginning to curl and brown. She wrenched out some weeds and plucked the heads from fading roses and dahlias until a noisy movement and hoarse whispers beyond the garden wall made her look up. She drew a breath in through her teeth and felt a twitch under one eye.

The youths were back with their foul language and their filthy habits. They took advantage of the darkening evenings to gather in the gloom behind the wall. Now she listened to the rough words and the silly giggles. She pictured their fawning and flirting, girls with bare midriffs and dreadful underwear, visible under tiny, teasing skirts. The crack and hiss of cans opening, the throaty laughter and simpering responses gave way to the quieter thrum of whispered embraces, the gulp and smack of wet kisses. Mabel pressed her ear against the wooden gate. Her flesh itched as she imagined young men with smiling mouths and slender hips, pawing at the plunging necklines and pert little bodies. The thought made her heart race and her cheeks flush.

She recalled her own youth; skirts were longer, necklines higher. She had never submitted to silly fancies. No man had dared to make leering advances towards her. Now, young men and women exposed their feelings through gestures and language. Unabashed and unconcerned they wrapped arms around waists, thrust hands in each other's pockets, mouths wet, tongues licking, desires unsuppressed. She shuddered, then allowed her breathing to quieten before pulling open the gate. Dark figures and quiet voices grew fainter as they retreated down the lane. The light let her down; all was indistinct. An empty lager can rolled back and forth on the ground. She kicked it away and retreated behind her own gate.

Late the following afternoon Mabel left her potions brewing in the attic. She put her canvas jacket on over her sweater and tweed skirt. Her gardening gloves covered her wrists and fitted closely against her arms.

She stepped out of her kitchen door into the little porch and paused beside the herbs flourishing in neat rows, the strange flowers captured and trained under her hands.

"Well now," she said as she pinched off a few weak leaves. "How are we today? You need some water, I see."

She trimmed and tended, soothed and watered until all was orderly. In the garden, she whispered encouragement to the foxgloves and the aconite, giving special attention to her clematis whose heart-shaped leaves hid its noxious spirit. She selected budding stems from several plants and placed them in a basket ready to take inside. She lingered for a while, listening to the traffic quieten out on the road, the starlings settle into the trees next door. The sun set and the moon rose but no sound drifted towards her from the other side of the garden gate. A worm of irritation wriggled up, but she pushed it down. There would be another time.

Safely inside the attic once again, the door locked against discovery and intrusion, Mabel ran fingers along pots and jars on busy shelves. She lifted a stopper and dark smoke whispered out, fading to pale green mist. She replaced the lid and sniffed the air, letting her mind grow calm. Sitting in her rocking chair, she reached for an ancient radio, looking for something to strengthen her resolve; something wild and pulsating that would continue to lift her spirits. The tuner found a familiar station and Mabel smiled with satisfaction. She relished the throaty screaming; the throbbing tones; the interjection of dialogue shouted at the world. What would it be like to be an iron maiden? She would have liked the power of a steely exterior to match those dark lyrics. How would it feel to be marked with the number of the beast?

She let her chair rock gently as the music pounded through her. A large spider spiralled lazily onto her arm. She crushed it between her finger and thumb, rubbing them together until the black, bloody threads fragmented.

*

The following evening, just as the red sun was once more lured towards the horizon, she looked out of the attic window. They were gathering again. She could hear them, laughing in intimate huddles, using her garden wall as a support for their embraces. The wind carried gasps of delight through the air. Mabel tapped gently on one or two jars. She flexed her fingers, then curled them into fists.

Hurrying out through the porch, she ignored her gardening jacket, and whispered, "Patience," to herself as she passed the rows of carefully nurtured pots. A breeze sidled past and bent the foliage towards her in little green nods. As she passed a withering rose bush, her skirt caught on a thorny stem. She reached down to snatch it away. Another stem caught on her sweater, clutching and tearing. She could hear the grunting laughter from behind the wall. Gasping with fury and frustration she wrestled the bush until it shed a flurry of brown-rimmed petals. She twisted from side to side but the thorns seemed to pulse with anger and resentment. With a final, violent wrench she freed herself and hurried down the garden, threads hanging from her skirt and sweater. By the time she opened the gate, the usual cluster of rubbish was all that remained; once again figures faded into the distance.

Mabel rasped out an angry sigh. A wide scratch on the back of her hand oozed thick red droplets around two black thorns. She sucked at the wound and withdrew the thorns with her teeth, spitting them onto the path and licking the blood. A drop lingered and dried at the corner of her mouth. She returned to the attic room and reached for her radio. She seethed and plotted. Finally, she breathed out and allowed the pounding in her head to be soothed by the vibrating rhythm of the music.

The next evening Mabel hurried down to the lane behind her garden and drew a smile at the group leaning against the wall. Three of the youths moved away. One boy waited as Mabel moved through the gate.

"Hello, Miss Thresher," he said. "We're not bothering you, are we?"

Mabel looked at the long hair, the tight jeans, the dark lines drawn under deeply blue eyes. She saw the instrument case he carried and the wild, heavy metal slogan on his tee-shirt. She lifted her head slightly and her eyelids fluttered as her mouth curled up in a wet, red smile. "Why no. Only, I've tried to catch — well, speak to you before but you always leave before I get the chance."

"Is something wrong?" His answering smile reached his eyes and her soul.

"I wonder if you could help me with something? It would only take a moment."

He turned to his friends — "Catch you later?" — then followed as Mabel led him through the garden, into the house and up the staircase to the attic. She indicated that he should go ahead and he smiled with delight at the boom of music emanating from the radio.

"Go on," she whispered. "I have something to show you."

He moved into the room and Mabel locked the door behind them.

David Betteridge

Successors

This surely was what you were created for,
To make this here a hereafter...
Mary Brooksbank

We stand on the top storey
of an Outlook Tower,
the skilled work of centuries.
It gives long vistas into history and place
that bring to mind our aching wish
always for *better*, sometimes *more*,
and our deep debt to those who stood
and looked and worked and wished
before.

The tower is sited on a dirt road
that leads to the land's far edge,
hazarded along the way by fire,
despair, fatigue, and dread.

History's better part,
only imagined now, lies farther still,
uncertain travelling ahead.

Seth Crook

April day arrivals

Ten greylag geese by the surf, spotted by a dachshund.
A triumphant boy, now a nine timeser at keepy-uppy.
Eight pied wagtails feeding in the beached kelp.
Seven loose family flocks of humans.
Six upturned drying kayaks, all of different colours.
Five stick figures in the sand, drawn with a smile.
Four red tips of paddles in action.
A tricycle enthusiastically powered by a small girl.
Two swans conversing.
One sun.

Seth Crook

The great escape

From breathlessness,
from despair.
From poverty,
from un-love.
From isolation,
from loneliness.
From ache.
From homelessness
shivering in a cardboard box.
From pettiness,
relentless pettiness.
From shame.
From circling in a concrete yard.
Under the wire,
over the wire,
in a tunnel from hut B12.
Under a wooden horse,
over a wooden horse.
With Captain X
and entire escape committee.
With JC,
or some other beardy Gandalf,
at the Harrowing of Hell.
With the boldest/baddest heroine
of THE cult classic movie,
to the happy land
glimpsed as the credits roll.
Everybody escapes.
Everyone.
Even the monster.

Derek Brown

Blue angel on Union Street

Out of all the blue angels
on Union Street
he was the bluest,
with his blue face
and his blue eyes
and his blue mouth
and his blue hands
and his blue clothes.

As if he had stepped
straight out of the bible
he stared into me
and through me,
his blue eyes unredeeming
the redeemed.
And the cars that passed
were not really there
and the clouds that passed
were not really there,
only unwieldy dimensions,
foolproof imperfections.

More than just sincere
he whispered in my ear
hints of unusual wisdom,
muses killed by sunlight,
evil-minded handmaidens,
April's disfigured shadows,
May's slowly dying warriors,
the fugitive loves of June,
the gaudy meteors of July,
strange entities of August,
September's new machines

and all that must come after,
what surely
must come after.
Out of all the blue angels
on Union Street
he was
undoubtedly
the bluest.

Mary Nixon

Intelligence test

There's this new boy called Ewan that's just come to our class. He is the most annoying boy ever. He's worse than Billy McFall and big Wullie put thegither. He shows off all the time. He says to Wullie,

"I could fight you — easy."

And when he says 'easy' he sort of hisses it right at Wullie's face then jumps back and starts dancing about throwing punches like the way you see the boxers on the telly. But Wullie's no' as daft as he looks.

"Aye? You — an who else? Get it, Ew-an?"

So every time he says he can do stuff better than everybody else, Wullie starts,

"You-an who else?"

Ewan even annoys the teacher. He says,

"In my old school we went on a trip every week." And, "In my old school I was a monitor." And then Miss McTavish jumps in with,

"They must really be missing you."

"They are," he says, and he's serious. He doesn't know sarcasm. He doesn't know Miss McTavish. So Friday afternoon, Miss McTavish says, "Who's up for a solo quiz challenge?"

Wullie wants to know if it's points or sweets for the prize.

"Points, William," says the teacher.

I remember the time she did Mastermind. She said the prize was a million points but we could do it as a team instead of individuals. None of us, even with three in a team, got any more than six questions right in the three minutes. But they were questions out a quiz book — Junior Edition it said on the cover. I can do better with the teacher's own questions.

"Pick me," says Ewan. "I was the quiz champion in my last school."

"Well, there's a surprise," says the teacher.

"We had a quiz team and a football team and the pitch was the size of —"

"Your mouth!" shouts Wullie.

"William, enough." And then she says, "Well, Ewan, here's your chance to show how smart you really are."

And he never got it. He didn't know the sarcastic voice. She usually keeps it for Wullie or Billy McFall. Even I've had it a few times. Ewan was smiling that I'm better than you lot smile he does. I know now where I've seen that kind of look and I know the right word that goes with it. My granny told me after we'd been talking to Mr Johnstone outside the butcher's. He thinks he's too good to live here and he always knows what's wrong with the world.

"He's so smug," says my granny. "Smug Mr Know-all."

Sssmug. That's Ewan. It's a great word. Trust my granny to know just the right word.

"Perhaps you'd like to sit at the front. How about my seat?" says Miss McTavish.

Well we knew then he was for it. Me and Sarah and Angela smiled to each other while Ewan sat out on the teacher's chair. It's one of they office chairs that you can put up or down. You can spin around on it as well. We sometimes do that at wet intervals when she's out the room. Ewan looks like he wants to twirl it round but he tries to sit still. He looks so smug but we all know he'll soon be knocked off his perch. My granny says that as well. And the best bit is that he doesn't even know it.

"So, are you ready, Ewan?" says Miss McTavish, sitting on a table up the back of the class.

"Yes Miss," he says, and I want to knock him right off the seat like the coconut shy you see in old films. Miss McTavish is speaking.

"Question one, Ewan: what goes in a toaster?"

"That's easy, toast."

"Bread goes in and toast comes out, Ewan," says the teacher.

That's one point to the teacher. We do a pretend tally mark in the air.

"Question two. Now this is a tricky one. First I want you to say silk five times."

Ewan says, "Silk silk silk silk silk," dead fast and loud.

"Now spell it," says the teacher.

"S, I, L, K," says Ewan.

"You're doing really well, Ewan. Now what do cows drink..."

"MILK!" he shouts. Then he looks smug.

Miss McTavish shakes her head slowly from side to side. "Oh Ewan, don't you know cows drink water?" And Ewan shakes his head in disbelief. That's two points to Miss McTavish. Me and Angela and Sarah do smug now and it's not finished yet. We know she's going to trick him but he can't see it.

"Question three, Ewan. Are you ready? Well, listen carefully. A red house is made of red bricks and a brown house is made of brown bricks, okay? So what..."

"A greenhouse is made of glass, ha ha, can't trick me anymore. My granda's got one."

"Oh dear, Ewan. You didn't let me finish the question. I was going to say — what holds the bricks together? We'll just go on with the next question. You might be luckier this time."

You could feel the silence. It was like we'd even stopped breathing, a film without the sound. Then the teacher spoke.

"Now Ewan, I know you've been really interested in the Home Front topic and you even went to the Imperial War Museum when your granddad took you to London. We heard all about it. You are quite an expert, so maybe this is just the question for you. If a British plane came down during World War Two when it was flying over France, tell me where would they bury the survivors?"

"Oh that's easy: France. There's lots of war graves in special cemeteries in France."

"No, Ewan. They didn't bury survivors, they took them prisoner."

Ewan's face crumpled. "Those are trick questions. I know all the capital cities in the world. I know all the colours of the rainbow. I know..."

Suddenly Ewan looked small and scared. He looked like he was trying not to cry, blinking his eyes fast. I do that sometimes. Miss McTavish knew it as well. She went to the shelf and got an Atlas.

"Very well, Ewan. Since you've just started your point chart I'll give you a real chance for fifty points. Capital cities."

And she started with the easy ones like Scotland, France, Italy, Germany, till he got his confidence back. Then she kept going, saying things like, "This is a bit trickier," and, "Take your time." She gave him twenty-five questions and he never made one mistake.

So she kept her word and gave him fifty points — two for each answer. He's still the most annoying boy next to Wullie and Billy McFall but I'll definitely pick him if I get to be captain of The Quiz Team.

David McVey

Kirkintilloch Co-operative, 1960s

Brass weights, like heavy golden chess pieces,
balance the bacon. It comes out one piece at
a time, one for each whisper of the hand-cranked
machine. Great trays of steak mince, raw wounds,
rub shoulders with pork shoulder and kidneys.
Beef ham waits to be sprinkled with dark silky spice
powder. More whispers; corned beef, slice by slice.

Golden bricks of butter are battered into shape
with weapons like ping-pong bats. Tamed,
they are robed in crinkling greaseproof paper.
For bread, we can have either plain or pan.
No one yet has invented 'artisan'.

Eiffel Towers, fruit slices and cream buns
are brought in flat wooden trays from
brown Co-op lorries. Tawny cairns of scones —
fruit and plain — rise on the counter.
"And some cheese," we said.
The choice is Cheddar — white or red.

Lynn Valentine

My mother's complaint when I moved north

'You're so far up the map now, I never know
where to look to find the weather at yours.'

Each time her children moved, my mother
tacked her heart to the TV weather map.

Imagined her offspring in their autumn coats
or shivering in the chill after the six o'clock news.

Weighted the places where she could find us,
tethered and tied us to her coordinates.

Located her son in the centre of things, held
my sisters' summers in the same spot as hers.

Mum, think if Scotland had a face, find the eye
where two firths meet and gild your love upon it.

I'll still find you when the chart grows dark
with only time and weather left to bind us.

Marie-Thérèse Taylor

As days grow long

We have been advised: it will sneak in under cover of darkness. Before daybreak, the call of the alarmed lark will fall on empty roads.

Mid-morning, transparent trees will stretch and leaf... Xylem tubes, with capillary compulsion, will fill with meltwater. An indignant hedgehog will be roused early from its winter bed to emerge with expectation, only to be disappointed...

Then the migraine.

By midday, the outraged sea will rise. Battered ships will pitch flotsam onto defenceless shores. Tides will reclaim gifts, still wrapped, from thankless children.

In the late afternoon, as if it were on caffeine, the earth will throw up shoots. Between rivers, the soil will soften.

By evening, only memories cover the ground. We will find consolation in reciting the names of herbs, but after this, what will there be to look forward to?

Someone will say: We need more time...

Not longer days.

Neil Beaton

Beslotted

As a teenager I became aware
of the coin machines, flashing
at the corner of the bar. Over eighteens only
with a balcony of buttons
to touch, nudge
an orchard of forbidden fruit.

I began to fondle the coins
into the slot
first one and then
as I mastered the Holds
everything I had banked
for years.

The more I fumbled
the greater the primal urge
to excite her flashing lights
to mingle with her jingles, until

one day, as I eased in everything I had
and the flutterings of her lights,
the frenzied ringing of her tintinnabulations
grew to a crescendo
I stabbed the Play button home
and the roulettes of fruit spun and spun
until they synched into a mighty payout ultimatum
and oh my god
pure silver flooded out, overbrimming the catch-tray.

The whole bar-room looked at me
in envy.

Now I play regularly.
Seventy-per-cent payout is my kind of
serendipity.

Neil Beaton

Black cat master

Casual in a lounge-suit he'll
make a killing at the casino, then
exit with disdain. He spits
at adversaries, hunts
in the underworld of thugs but
remains a gentleman, pitch-perfect
at one with the dark.

Undertaker in mourning clothes he'll
stroll through your secrets
sharpen his blades as he
walks all over you, lies down
on the rumble-strips of your ribs.
With his nine passports he can
infiltrate a hedge, a barn, a country
neutralise assassins, play roulette with
his divided loyalties.

Frontiers are hurdles he'll
ghost his way through. He'll
sleep soundly with the enemy when
he's had his way with you.

Morag Anderson

Kintsugi

As the ochre fleck in her right eye fades
I unhinge golden hoops from still soft lobes.
With the delicacy of horology
curve the memory of her warmth,
vital as the weight of a bee,
through my own ears.

Careful not to crease the stained sheet
that hides her wounds, I press against her
as she cools. The transfer of heat:
a red-hulled ship breaking ice fields.
She seals my fractures
with seams of hot gold.

Tom Gillespie

Eulogy

Father died today, or it might have been yesterday, I'm not sure. I got an email from Janie, but it was buried in my spam folder for some reason. All it said was Father passed away. The funeral is on Friday. That could mean anything, maybe it was this morning. I don't know.

I haven't spoken to Janie for over three years, so it was a bit of a surprise to hear from her. We lost touch when she emigrated to Australia, and then when Father moved out of Dennistoun that was the end of that.

I don't think I'll be going to the funeral. I can't see the point. They'll all be there, waiting to start in at me again. They're the ones who should be apologising. I don't know where all that bitterness and rage comes from. They need to take a long hard look at the mess they've made of their own lives before they start in at me. I mean, the way they go on, anyone would think that I was the bad guy in all of this.

I could send a wreath, but he'd have thought that was too sentimental. Or maybe I could email a few words to Janie and she could read them out at the service. But what would I say? What is there to say?

I knew he'd been ill for a while. His sister mentioned something about it in a Christmas card a couple of years ago. I suppose I should have made the effort to go and see him but I just couldn't face it. And anyway, we'd only have ended up back where we were, and that's no good to anyone.

Tom Gillespie

I stand witness

The boy was ten years old, but that was only a guess. Nobody knew who he was or where he came from, or why he did what he did. At first his behavior went unnoticed. I mean, who's going to spot a small kid in amongst the hordes of tourists, commuters and passers-by. They just walked on, too busy pushing and pulling themselves through the rituals of their own struggles with life. Some say it went on for a month, but it might have been longer. One day he just showed up, and so it began and so it went on. At 7.56 a.m. he would appear from nowhere, and find his spot in the heart of Times Square. Straightening his back, and standing on his toes, he would stretch and twist his neck at a strange angle, and fix his gaze upon the clock tower at the top of the Paramount building. He would hold that position for precisely twenty-four minutes, and at 8.20, he would turn 180 degrees and set off at a pace towards Central Park and the Upper West Side.

After a few days, the frequency of his appearances began to attract the attention of a few regulars, who passed by at the same time each morning on their way to their daily grind. By the end of the first week, a shop assistant finally stopped to ask him his name and what he was doing, but he ignored her and continued his vigil. Halfway through the second week, the woman was so concerned about him, she called the police, but by the time they arrived he had already gone. A local journalist picked up the story, and wrote a short piece for the Wall Street Journal entitled *The Boy In Waiting*, and within hours of its publication, the media descended on the square to capture the boy in action. But still, the boy continued in silence. Soon, plots were hatched and tales concocted, and photographs and footage appeared on social media sites. Television producers and chat show hosts whispered six-figure offers in the boy's ear for exclusive rights. Yet despite extensive media campaigns and public appeals, the boy's identity remained a mystery. And even when he was followed, he always managed to elude his pursuers and disappear into the labyrinth of back alleys and passageways of Manhattan.

But then, in the dying moments of his final day of pilgrimage, the boy slowly raised his left arm, and extending his index finger, pointed up towards the sky. And in that instant, the rays of the ascending sun penetrated the forest of concrete and steel surrounding the square, and Paramount's old clock face exploded in a dazzling display of white light and heat. The crowd clapped and cheered, and rubbed their eyes in amazement. But when they turned back to congratulate the boy on his immaculate timing, he was nowhere to be seen. Fighting his way through the pandemonium, the Wall Street reporter who had been following the story from the start stepped up to the spot where the boy had stood for a month or more. And searching the ground, he discovered a tiny finger-wide hole in the tarmac. After a few minutes of prodding and probing, first with a pencil, and then with one of his house keys, a small spherical object popped out of the aperture and bounced between the legs and feet of the curious bystanders. The reporter gave chase and the crowd followed behind as it rolled across the square. But the object was too quick and when it reached the far side, it rattled off the curb and came to an abrupt halt. And before the exhausted reporter could reach his elusive prize, a young girl escaped from the tight grip of her mother's hand and snatched it up.

Everyone stopped.

The girl looked at the object and back at the crowd, and holding it aloft she cried out, "A star!" But in her excitement, she let it slip from her fingers, and it dropped through the grate of a drain and disappeared into the sewer.

That was the end of it. The boy never returned to his spot on Times Square, his identity was never traced, and the strange object was never found. In the days that followed, there was talk of further sightings of the boy in various parts of the city, but none of them were ever confirmed or documented. And after a while the story was forgotten and the world moved on.

But sometimes, in the wee small hours of my night, when I think about him standing there, day after day, like a shadow caught in the dazzling glare of the early spring sunshine, I have come to realize that he wasn't the boy in waiting at all. The truth is, we were all waiting for him.

Jo Gilbert

Condorman (1981)

Chattering the whole walk
every second step a skip
fuelled by excitement
a rare cinema trip
small hand held
in father's spade grip

He lifts a digit to his lips
as the house lights dim
she pays most attention
to his North Sea
battered face
lit by the flickering reel

Each line, each mark
shaped by whisky and graft
she hears the waves in his breath
he's fluid and dangerous
yet more set
than anyone she knows

Her heart bobs along
like a buoy on a wave
never taking her gaze
from her father's face
smiling, despite not knowing
a thing about the film

Jo Gilbert

Stanley

He telt mi nae ti pick it up — ah nivver listen
dinna like gettin telt fit ti di
aye, she'll be led but she winna be telt
ma Granda sais aboot me

Ah liked the blue o the hunnel
an the sharp triangle stickin oot
wis like a jewel, forbidden
it hid ti be mine

Da's growl fae the door
geid ma a hoor o a fear
an Stanley fell, slicin
recht through ma saft palm

Sae sharp it wisna sare
until the bleed started runnin
bit a wisna greetin
ah'd a morbid fascination
wi the sight o blood gushin

Mony years later
ah'd crave for at feelin
Stanley's a wye o copin
ma best pal for openin

ma skin, ti see if ah still bleed
so ah ken am alive
an nae deid

Emma Baker

Dreams

I dream I am a writer.
A dynamic thinker soon to birth an epic;
a work so richly textured and subtly rendered
it moves the masses, thrills the critics, cleanses the world.

Spoken of in the same breath as Atwood, Shields, Mantel.
A fresh voice. Witty and erudite. Poignant and penetrating.

I wait, pen poised over lined sheet.
My fingers tingle, awaiting revelation.
I envisage invention flooding from the nib,
crowding the page with provocative plots,
scathing satire, astute analogies.

Characters queue to audition for their big break
but are cast aside by stinging judgements.
Lofty themes wade through a mire of doubt
searching for an escape route onto the page.
Plots open, develop and fade,
swept on a sea of expectation.

It is just a dream, I sigh.
I remain cemented to this reality.

So I reach back
to summer streets bubbling with palpable dreams,
to chalk-marked rainbow playgrounds,
when a trickling burn became a mighty river with one thought,
a pebbledash wall became a cliff to be scaled in a single leap,
when frog spawn was pixie pearls,
a clothes-horse a castle,
a tree a whole kingdom.
When dreams merged with reality
and to journey between them was effortless.

Then, I became lost in writing
so that when Mrs Taylor called 'Time' I was jolted from reverie,
amazed to awaken unscathed from my adventure
in the world of desks, chalk and screeching bells.
When the red pen proclaimed 'Excellent!'
I did not doubt it.
I was peerless.
And as I walked from the classroom,
I slipped seamlessly into my next dream.

Now, as I wait, pen poised, fingers tingling,
I close my eyes hoping to capture that child,
and hitch a ride into her dreams.

Emma Baker

A letter to my body

As a child you were skinny and smooth.
Strong, sleek, straight-edged.
Uncomplicated.
A minimalist design,
with licence to stand proudly topless
on my bunk-bed tree-house
and roar Tarzan's primal cry.

You were Spiderman, Batman, The Hulk.
A brave soldier saving a lost world.
You held no shame.
Poker thin — straight up and down —
you declared neither *Male* nor *Female*
just effortlessly carried me
fizzing with future.
Fearless.

Then you got complicated.
Clean strong edges dissolved.
Your outline blurred as you bulged unwanted flesh
in hard-to-hide places.
Oozing and leaking
you transformed.
An unruly package
stuffed into flesh-flattening elastic.

Now, you roared *FEMALE*
with unabashed glee.
But I could not share your joy.
The strap pinged in Science,
a stinging wound
deepening my growing paranoia
of what you, my *new* body,
were telling the world about *me*:

What I could and could not do;
who I could and could not be.
You said I could be Jane,
but not Tarzan; M.J,
but not Spiderman.
The Damsel, the bride, the love interest,
The prop.

Emma Baker

Our child

In Italy we first dreamt you.
Spoke you out of dust on drifting summer strolls
through winding Venetian streets.
We sketched your outline on gnarled chattering tables
and drank your laughter in long gulps of blood red Chianti.
On the dark sands of the Lido we moulded your future
as the green lagoon whispered its glistening promise.

Back home, the grey screen sketched your outline — still.
Silent.
A promise broken.

So, on bitter November nights we draw blankets round,
and howl to the wind for our lost dream.
Curled tightly together
we paint you with our longing,
bright as Italian sun on shimmering sea.
We close our eyes and strain
to hear the murmured oath of its waves once more.

Summer returns and we emerge,
soles soaked in morning dew.
Under cool warmth of sunrise
still we wait
patiently
for you.

Jane Lamb

Orkney spring

Spring comes to the islands late and slow;
what sparse and stunted trees there are, keep low
beneath the constant wind;
the cow parsley frosting the hedgerow,
May blossom waiting until June to bloom,
hesitating in the sun's weak glow,
then scattering snow around the fields,
where newborn lambs will grow
in the lengthening days.

Swara Shukla

Blind faith

You call it cowardice, I know. For me though, these shadows here, swathing us from violent eyes — this is where I feel the bravest.

I know what valiance constitutes for you: street brawls, love declarations atop thatched roofs — acts of grandiosity that you have the luxury to emulate from all those Bollywood movies you get so (endearingly) excited about.

I don't blame you for wanting more. For wanting to walk out of this hidden corner of stolen kisses and clandestine whispers and hold hands while eating kebabs at Iqbal *chacha*'s stall like the marrieds get to do.

I don't blame you because I want all those things too.

Sneaking you in small secret doses, crossing thresholds after the dark declares it forbidden, wrapping my burqa tighter to claim its anonymity for myself, snaking around piss-filled streets to find you in the corner behind the school; these are my grand gestures. However finite, however rushed — these moments here in the shadows with you are laden by a weight I carry into sleepless nights, into every excuse that I manage to churn out to Amma and Baba without stuttering, into every jolt of paranoia I tamp down when the footsteps behind me sound too much like my brother's every time I make my way towards you.

I feel strong in these shadows because I take so many leaps here. Across lines dividing faiths and religions; lines between bravery and cowardice; between sanctity and blasphemy.

I realise how weightless these moments are for you, how fleeting, how insufficient. My sporadic strength would never be enough in the face of your brawn.

What you think of as reassurances, cementation of a possible (impossible) future for us — *I will come and ask for your hand, I will fight your parents and mine, I will fight for us* — are just corrosive to the fight I am putting up; they exclude me from the equation altogether because they don't make space for prospects of more whip-marks marring my back, of being shipped off to one of those unknown bridal homes I lost Zainab to. This fear is a part of me, hammered in constantly for twenty-one years — you can't wrench it out with words heralding a fight both you and I are incapable of.

You are too sure in your love. Too sure in your perception of it as some universally panacean sentiment that I am sure your temples and your scriptures paint it as. And that is what I blame you for. For failing to see the glaring differences between your gods and your heroes, and the blinded humans swarming the smelly streets of this town.

You don't have the protective cover of fear. You didn't have to grow up with it. I tried to give you mine, but you wouldn't take it.

My fear will have to protect you.

I will stop blaming you soon. It is just what this town does to its people, I think. Blinds them with their own faith, their unwavering conviction in fragile things. I tried to defy them with you. I wish I didn't have to defy you too.

Defiance is my only constituent of strength. So, I will have to bid you goodbye. A quiet one, unvocal — like how everything else is with me.

You turned out to be my destined failed uprising. Everyone here gets one. I hope you never get to have yours.

Alun Robert

Raisin Edzell Blues

Anither autumnal mornin dark, dank. Forebodin.
Slender mellow crescent visible tae the educated eye.
Streets lichts hummin orange, flickerin above slick cobbles.
Been rainin through the nicht, forecast for mair later.
Nae surprise there then but it's dry for the noo.

Toonser tattie howkers clad in tartan scarves, coats, wellies.
There's mithers suckin Woodbines tuggin wee bairns grumpy
emergin frae grey tenements aff sprawlin council estates;
the armies o ants armed wi lunch pieces o ate-able fodder
concocted in the scullery frae left ower suppers, cald.

Passin shift workers saunterin hame. Knackered, downtrodden.
Barely compos mentis but relieved at nae signin on the Bru.
Yet nae intense debates twixt brother an blood brother
aboot politics, aboot fitba or the burden o hire purchase
or aboot parochial trivia at this ungodly time.

As dark blue diesel camels crawl oot frae the corp depot,
hardly a Morris Minor or Ford Consul purrin in sicht, on site.
Then howkers hoovered up intae double-decker Leylands
for a journey out tae sodden fields in the nearby carse.
Some sittin, some standin for near on twenty minutes.

Another day o hard labour for a modest wage (addin
tae a household income threatened by rampant mechanisation)
tae buy bairns fresh clobber tae see them through the winter
with the surplus assigned tae a weekly Christmas budget club.
For there micht be a Noel this year, God willin.

Lang day at the coal face wi a cadre o sisters. Camaraderie
crackin at the seams; haein a crack when they can.
Pickin frae a field yardage, measured oot by teuchter foremen —
shorter for wifies profferin a wink, smile and a raucous yelp —
while half bits for each bairn until they reach puberty.

Then as the local village kirk strikes up tae seven-thirty
scatterin massed black rooks in vulture-esque swoops,
round comes a Massey Fergie diggin up blue tatties.
Scatterin them on virgin soil. The jewels tae be gathered
by toonser howkers poised in linear vectors tae the horizon.

For hoor upon hoor battlin agin prevailin south-westerlies
grimacin wi back pains worse than in pregnancy, they claim,
raisin bulbous Edzell Blues for a market doon south where
the vicissitude o desperate economies is scarcely understood
in an autumnal mornin dark, dank. Forebodin.

Derek Crook

MacDougall's art studio and garage

This is his installation,
his life's hymn
to human creativity.

See him in his workshop doorway
staring critically at his pumps,
no spattered smock but padded boilersuit,
greased boot-tip to woolly cap,
surveying his alternative approach
to Sistine Chapels.
A Hebridean Michelangelo.

That Volvo balanced on that Viva —
is the composition right?
The top two inches to the left perhaps?
The rust on that old tractor wheel —
perhaps the red needs deepening
but the light
is not the same as yesterday
and light, of course, is outwith any man's control.

One drop of oil would spread iridescence
on that pot-hole pool, but how to get it,
oh how to get it exactly, exactly right?

A critic in a pearly Peugeot
slides sleekly to a pump
and spoils the composition utterly.

But not for long.

Derek Crook

Looking out of a train window

The green wheat sea
washes indolently westward
periscoped by power poles
in line astern.

No crooked idiosyncrasy
of shrub or tree
argues against the regularity,
the symmetry
of punctuated summer greenery.

Someone has left
their magazine behind.
The model's face is perfect so
I give her a moustache
and reconsider my position
on graffiti.

Sharon Boyle

Glass drunk dry

We all had our hobbies: I was passionate about books; Ma was into her dancing; Dad toyed with DIY, and Auntie May lived to torment the life out of me.

"I was a wanted baby," she crooned one time the whisky got a hold of her. "A wanted baby. Unlike you, Heather. Your Mammy did a terrible thing and trapped your father. You," she waved her finger across my eleven-year-old face, "you were most decidedly and assuredly unwanted."

I relayed this unsettling news to my parents the next day at breakfast, the need for rebuttal in my voice. There was none forthcoming. Ma came round the table to give me a hug and Dad withdrew his spoon from his mouth to say, "Your auntie's a nutter. There's not an attic in the country big enough for her."

I later heard him say to Ma, "Your sister's getting worse. Have a word."

This was true. Auntie May had been classed by the doctor as an invalid, a word that turned into three whenever she used it. Her curse of weak, chalky bones was our curse too.

I mulled over Dad's attic-logic — a place to keep nutters; a hidey-hole to spare family blushes. I was impressed he shared the same opinion as the fabulous Charlotte Brontë but concerned that, like the original and true Mrs Rochester, it was me and not Auntie May who slept in the converted attic. Was it possible to slip into mental feebleness in a sugar-pink room full of books and Barbies?

"I want to move, Dad. The air in my room isn't healthy. Sometimes I feel the vapours coming over me."

He was laying a path in the garden. "Vapours? Where d'you hear that tripe? In one of those highfalutin books?" He soaked up forehead sweat with the wrist of his jumper. "Try working in a mechanics workshop and you'll know all about unhealthy air."

Ma was as useless. When I suggested the possibility of a room swap, she gave a chancy look. "Your Auntie May cannae handle the stairs."

"She's not a Dalek. What if there's a fire? How will I get out?" Although I asked this to test her love, it was a genuine worry and one that was now successfully transferred.

I heard my parents that night through the thin floor of my bedroom.

"We'll install fire alarms," soothed Dad.

"So we'll be up in time to watch our daughter frazzle but not to actually save her?" Ma was great on the histrionics front. A thick streak of it ran in the family: her, Auntie May and apparently me.

"I'm not moving up there," Auntie May declared to Ma the next morning in the kitchen. "Those stairs are like bloody Everest. Besides, we agreed the sleeping arrangements in the beginning, if you remember. It's that husband of yours you want to harangue. Could he not have put a decent set of stairs in — one the council folks would pass?"

"What utter shite, May," sheeshed Dad, springing up from the couch and bounding through. "If you didnae drink so much you'd find those stairs possess a normal gradient."

"Possess a normal gradient? Who talks like that? I'll tell you, a third rate shyster of a builder. I'll have you know I imbibe for medicinal purposes, for I am an In Va Lid."

"I'm not having Heather cooped up there sparking to death," said Ma to Dad. "You'll need to do something."

The next week Dad dragged the trampoline across the back lawn to beneath my bedroom. He instructed me on the new safety catch he had hammered into the window and pantomimed the act of bounding forth from said window onto the trampoline below.

I was not impressed. Even Mrs Rochester died plummeting onto honest hard stone. "Will it support my weight from this height?"

"This is a converted bungalow, Heather, not the Empire State Building. You'll be fine." End of conversation and concern.

*

Six years later Auntie May's wasting bone disease had still not killed her. It was true she could no longer doddle about the garden, but her spongy frame still allowed sly excursions to the drinks cabinet.

Dad would mutter, "She's neither a half glass full or empty. She's a glass drunk dry."

Like a prisoner nearing release, I checked off my calendar waiting for the day I would attend university, leave the overpopulated house and escape Auntie May's snides.

"So what does the princess want for going to yoonie?" she asked over supper and gin.

"Money for digs, ta."

"You're not staying at home?" Dad.

"I just cannae believe they'd let someone like you into one of those yoonie places." Auntie May.

"You know fine well I've always had As."

"It's perhaps for the best." Ma.

"Aye." Dad. "Get away from the unhealthy air in here."

"And where's the money coming from to support her?" Auntie May. "You two never knew how to take care of anything, including money."

Cash slipped through the household coffers like water cascading down the hills after a first thaw. Auntie May was the one with money, earned from a long-ago, middling bestseller that proved decent enough on the royalties front. Occasionally she relented and scattered a few pennies around. But not this time. My paltry student grant required a massive top-up she refused to furnish.

"For the love of God, Auntie May, I'll study best if I have a place in town."

She let the booze swirl in her glass and gave a tight smile, letting the words unwanted baby neon up in her eyes. I stared at her. The spiteful blood that flowed in her veins also flowed in mine. I would remember this day.

I enrolled at university and buckled down to extended days of travelling. A month after matriculation Auntie May spent a fortune on converting the garage into a games room. "To keep that father of yours out the body of the house."

She purchased a pool table and smirked at me over its baize as we all herded into the room to inspect the thing. Dad, his pride well and truly bought, racked the balls.

"Shall we have a wee tester now?" He lifted the wooden triangle. "I'll break." He lent low, chin to cue and gave the balls a firm whack. He closed his eyes, chin still on cue and never regained consciousness.

As far as I was concerned it was Auntie May and not the high stodge /no exercise combo that finished him off. I ignored her for the duration of my three-year course in which I graduated with honours, securing the post of a grand paying job in Edinburgh. I announced to Ma my intention of renting a place in the city.

Ma's throat bobbed like an ostrich's. "Don't go. Heather, I cannae deal with your Auntie May's bitterness anymore."

"Why don't you chuck her out?"

She shook her head. "I don't have the heart. Besides, both me and your dad promised to look after her."

I sighed. I shrugged. I stayed. At least my new office had the distraction of bristling, competitive men. I bagged one of the less self-serving in my first month.

"No way am I taking you home," I said after three months of togetherness. "Not to a fussing mother and a mad, dipso aunt. You'll meet them at the wedding." I blanched as he smiled. I had been joking.

A year later, James convinced me to step up the aisle. The day would have been perfect if Dad had been present and Auntie May not. I made friends with a bottle of wine to surmount her sidelong glances and staggered through the first dance as if the floor was made of butter. Ma was as proud as a show-horse.

It was a shame, then, that during my honeymoon Ma, giddy on drink, according to Auntie May, had attempted to extinguish a small fire in the kitchen, "that spit could've put out." She tried to smother it with the fire blanket Dad had installed on the wall years earlier. The blanket wouldn't pull free and by the time Auntie May hobbled through, Ma was "scorched to a charred lump. The only things untouched were her dancing feet."

I survived the funeral in a haze of pills. As we piled from the church I overheard Auntie May say, "She was already cremated, I don't know why we needed another," and knew I needed to be far away from her.

James agreed. "We'll sell the house and never have to see your odious bitch aunt again."

In order to sell, we moved into the house to oversee the professionals who rebuilt the kitchen and rectified my father's more determined DIY projects. The day we banged in the For Sale sign was the day I discovered I was pregnant. James bristled at the poor timing.

"We're not in our own place. We're residing with our own Baby Jane Horror who smirks, cackles and screeches at all hours. Jesus." He left, scuffing past Auntie May who had been loitering in the hallway.

"Watch the bones, fella!" She shambled into the lounge, her mouth flat-lining. "A baby, eh? That'll be the end of our peace."

"Start looking for your own place, you have your own money," I said, wiping my eyes. "In the meantime you'll have to go into the attic. Your room will be the nursery."

"Pardon me?"

"The house needs loads of work. Who knows when we'll sell. Could take months."

"What about my porous bones?"

"There's always sheltered housing."

She recoiled like a snake. "All right, I'll take that attic room and let everyone know what you're doing. Trying to finish me off with a set of death-defying stairs."

"I'm getting rid of that rusted trampoline," I said. "If you one day decide to leave by a window you should at least have the dignity of falling onto a concrete path."

Her face changed. She sucked in a long stream of air. "You," she pointed. "You, your mother, your father. You all took from me."

"You're delusional. I've no idea why my parents put up with you. You made Dad's life a misery."

"As he did mine!" she screeched.

"My parents bent over backwards for you. Sometimes they put you first. Over me!"

"And so they damn well should've." She came closer. "I saw him first. He was mine. I even fell pregnant by him."

I stepped back, away from her hands waving in the air, fingers splayed, like a demented pianist's.

Her eyes filled with tears. "And it was a wanted baby. It would have been a very much loved baby."

Her wail was horrible. I covered my ears and hurried from the room.

After a few moments, as I stood at the bathroom sink, I heard her mooch along the hall; heard her faltering climb of the stairs as she eased her soft bones against the banister — bones that had been unable to carry her child.

I placed my hands on my swell, the place where my unfinished baby was quietly growing, filling my womb, stretching my skin and flooding my body with cut-throat, defensive hormones. I nodded at my reflection in the bathroom mirror. I had a new hobby now and there was no room for a decidedly unwanted relative.

Sharon Boyle

I do not like thee, Doctor Fell

— but I keep the reason wrapped close about me like layers of petticoats. It would not be seemly for me to mention how Doctor Fell investigates his patients' ailments. Not a stitch of clothing can be present for him to successfully deduce the malady.

"I have no malady," I told him.

He made a noise that implied I spoke nonsense; that as a young woman I should not question a medical man but instead stand quiet and humble.

"You are in danger," he advised, wiping his mouth — his ill-fitting teeth making him leak saliva. "Not of the physical kind, not yet, but your mental weakness will seep into your corporeal being, and worse, into your spiritual."

He said I possessed a hatred of my father, proved by refusing to pray when my father asked. He had studied mental fortitude, he told me, and lack of it, in his job as medical keeper at Bedlam. "I am a man who seeks out the truth," was his boast.

Thomas Blood, thief of King Charles's jewels, had been one of his patients. Doctor Fell described how he insisted on Mr Blood's body being exhumed — Mr Blood being a known trickster who had possibly faked death to escape punishment. I think if Mr Blood had faked death it was to escape Doctor Fell.

"I do not like thee, Doctor Fell," I said. "I do not wish thee to visit."

"It is pleasing you do not like me, Elizabeth, for it means you will not try to impress me; that what I see is your true nature and not the pretence women often present to men."

He continued to visit and I continued to lay bare the truth of my revulsion, jolting and jigging every time he traced a finger on my cheek or wisped a hand through my hair.

An alarming rumour sprang up that he needed a wife. But I discovered it was no rumour when he next visited and gave me a primrose-yellow shawl and the news that my father had blessed our engagement. It was at this point I decided I did hate my father.

"It will be better," said Doctor Fell, "to bide with me so I may care for you, otherwise you may have to be cared for — elsewhere."

"You mean — Bedlam?"

He nodded slowly. "That is where wilful girls go who cannot accept what is best for them. It is where they rightfully belong." He took my hand and puckered a wet kiss onto it as I prayed to God to grant my skin the quills of a hedgehog.

That night I walked to the river, slipped off my shoes and swam to the other side, ensuring to entangle the yellow shawl among the reeds.

All this is history — happenings of two years and seven months past. I now teach piano and French to three girls in a quiet part of the neighbouring county. My plan was to return home once Doctor Fell married, claiming memory loss from shock at my near drowning, and a recent and gradual recovery of it. But only yesterday a rumour reached me that Doctor Fell remains in a worrying and dangerous state: bachelorhood. He is apparently broken-hearted at the loss of his betrothed, and despite general encouragement to embolden himself against grief and take up with another, he still searches for her body. Doctor Fell is a determined seeker of the truth — this I know and know full well.

Sharon Boyle

Clay-cladded hearts

She kept him wet and malleable: smoothing the crook of his legs; the spread of his chest; his ears, set close to his head like a baby's; his lips, puttied into fullness.

She stepped back. "Your mouth — finished."

He twitched and broke apart his lips, the clay pocking. *And my eyes?*

"The moulding's there. I'll do the pupils last."

I want to see myself now.

"Later." She pressed clay onto his cheeks.

And what happens to me when I'm finished?

"You've been commissioned for an exhibition."

Perhaps I don't want to be exhibited.

"And miss all that attention? Like hell."

Does the exhibition explain this pose?

The statue was kneeling, a cocky tilt to its head, one arm thrown up, fingers splayed.

"You're casting me off. Art reflecting life." She paused. "I've left you naked."

Were you thinking of hiding my pride and your joy? Of course I must be nudo.

He came from Shropshire but peppered his talk with Italian, thinking it artistic.

"We were good together, especially when nudo."

The first few years. After that all bodies grow dull.

Wrong. Clay or flesh, she could gaze a while at a body, returning to it years after, retaining appreciation, marvelling at how its essence changed. When she'd kept vigil at the hospital bedside after his car accident, she memorised his comatose contours and quirks. Until Julia turned up.

Chiselled and proportioned, Julia had shimmied a hand under the covers.

"She wanted —" a chorus of plosives "— to see if you still worked."

You slapped her. Ruined my climax.

She picked up the needle, ready to prick pupils.

*

The plaque over the gallery door reads EXHIBITION ON DESERTION. Soft-footed visitors murmur and nod.

He kneels centre-stage, refusing to interact. She perches on the bench opposite remembering when he'd spewed apologies down the phone, insisting Julia was transitory. She'd gone to collect him. With one leg out the car she watched Julia escort him in his wheelchair from hospital. Afterwards, she drove home and smashed every model of him, weeping staccato sobs over the powdered ashes. She heard later that Julia walked out, refusing to act nursemaid — proving he was the transitory one.

She studies him. The raised arm? The head angle? The still-unpricked eyes?

The statue is beseeching, begging: *Don't leave.*

She approaches and leans in, whispering, "Ciao."

Hamish Scott

Rael warlds

Thare is a warld ayont wir wits
wir mynd can no uptak
an yet this unkent warld sae rael
as onie proven fack

Paula Nicolson

Chippies are always shut on Sundays

We moved into the first floor flat on a Tuesday. It wasn't the best or the worst day to move. Mum normally moved on Sundays, but the chippy was always shut on Sundays in England, so we took to moving on Tuesdays.

'Uncle Dan', my mum's latest boyfriend, had taken the day off work to help us. But he paid more attention to Mum than moving stuff.

He shouted at me, "Pull your finger out," when I sat down for a rest. And so, when he wasn't looking, I took his coat, climbed the stairs, and stuffed it down the rubbish chute.

It was last spotted being worn by an old homeless guy, shuffling his trolley down the street.

Sue Proudlove

Safe place

When I feel beaten down,
pursued
by hate
and other people's anger
and my own shame,
I find myself longing
to put one foot in front of the other

left   right

keep   going

don't look back, don't stop
to pick up your belongings,
don't run but look for the nearest exit,
leave the building,
and instead of assembling in the car park
just keep walking.

Better still if no one sees me go.
If nobody follows, I'm free.
Keep my head down
and lean into the wind.
My safe place
is where I can sink into the walls
and let the thoughts in my head flow
cool and clear
like a stream on its way to the sea.

Sue Proudlove

Snow in Venice

This unexpected stranger
settles softly
blurs the lines
makes features indistinct.

The city waits
breath held
sound muffled
familiar yet never seen like this.

Your face too
has changed
since we came in summer heat and clamour
when the crowds held us close.

Your grief holds you
frozen
waiting for the chill to pass.

Aileen Paterson

Listen

My language is the wind through the trees
the rustling of leaves
the sound of the sea.

My language is birdsong
the land awakening in spring
the opening of daffodils.

My language is the thawing of snow
into fast flowing rivers
the silence of standing stones.

My language is the beating of a blackbird's wings
the song of the earth
and the quiet music of everything.

Aileen Paterson

Wings

What begins as pain
is only the start of it.
The losses
will tether you to the earth
pinning the wings
you have all but forgotten.
Love does this.
But one starry night
under an autumn moon
you will fly
to the topmost branches
of the tallest tree
and you will sing.

Greg Michaelson

Still not still

Left arm, right arm:
kicking, breathing.

Stiff in the shoulders;
sore in the hips.

Counting strokes.
Counting lengths.

I still feel young
in this anxious old body.

Out on the front,
and round on the back.

I'm my body,
but my body's not me.

Left arm, right arm:
kicking, breathing.

Where have I come from?
Where am I going?

Counting strokes.
Counting lengths.

Family? Friends?
Where have they gone?

Out on the front,
and round on the back.

We remember them,
as they fade away.

Left arm, right arm:
kicking, breathing.

But who will ever
remember us?

Counting strokes.
Counting lengths.

We'll soon be ghosts
for our grandchildren's children.

Out on the front,
and round on the back.

All we can do
is remember each other.

Still counting.
Still kicking.
Still breathing.
Still not still.

Ann MacKinnon

Out at sea

Now that he is ninety he talks.
Such a torrent is let loose.

The crew lined the decks
while drowning men begged for life.

These souls, like corks bobbing
beside the ship, had to be forsaken.

Some were saved,
given food and clothes,

ploughed back to a safe shore
far from their shipmates.

He has nightmares
about the lost ones,

singing to be saved,
but there was no room.

He felt depth charges, explosions
but that night haunts him still.

He looks at the old photos,
glad for the few they saved

but mourning the lost,
still out at sea.

Ann MacKinnon

On the way to Skye

Before I came to Kyle
I thought the name a fairytale —
Lochalsh.

Delivered by train to this place —
white — overlooked by Five Sisters,
black as nuns' cloaks.

My bag lies unopened
on a golden counterpane
as I stare from the window.

Castle Moil is sharp, stark —
then gone as cloud covers it —
lost in greenery.

The smell of new paint,
seawrack and salt
sifts my senses.

The eider on the wall is still
but outside all is movement
as boats vie for places.

Once it was the bonnie boat
that sped us to Skye
but now it is a span of silver steel.

A C Clarke

Poppies

spring out of a soldier's eye. Don't let people tell you
their red is blood-colour.

Blood is the colour of the orlop deck
where Nelson staged his exit.

Bloodshed's metaphors come sugared
with the sentiment of drums,

cavalry charges, sea-battles picturesqued
in canvas after canvas.

Did men surrounded by the gassed, the trampled,
the blown to fragments,

see any other colour than khaki
horizon to horizon?

Flowers would have been welcome.
Live red flowers.

A C Clarke

Loch Thom revisited

[Italicized words are from W S Graham's poem *Loch Thom*]

Up near Loch Thom on the path where municipal verse
adorns a scrollwork bench looking out to the same
stretch of your childhood you went back to —
did you or was it in dream? — and found it
colder than you remembered, I pause and use
your eyes for a moment. Still unfarmed land
though sheep potter among the tussocks,
still, sometimes, a curlew's cry.

You worded this landscape into its full existence.
No-one after is going to come close.
Your lines should be carved here, not platitudes.

I picture you at the water's edge scanning for fish
on a knifewind day, all your dead past crowding
in shoals around your stillness, Greenock a grimy
tumble of houses below, the *blue moors
of Ayrshire* away beyond the bowl in the hills
where west coast rain gathers and gathers.
You raise your head and stare into that distance,
listening. I hear nothing but the sigh of the wind.

Your shoulders jerk as if they flinched.
You turn. I watch your back recede
shrink to minnow size before
you step out of my vision. *Farewell.*

Alan Gillespie

The permanent arrangement of Lilli Crabtree

Lilli studied her face in the mirror. She raised her eyebrows half an inch, flared her nostrils ever so slightly, and pushed her tongue against the roof of her mouth. Much better.

It was half past eight in the morning. Lilli's first class started in one hour. Her first class *ever*. She still wasn't sure how she'd blagged the job of yoga instructor at the community centre. They'd seemed overly excited that she owned her own yoga mat. Then, when she'd demonstrated the Downward Facing Dog — the only pose that guaranteed she wouldn't fall over — they'd clapped and whistled and asked if she could start a week on Monday.

"I don't mean to sound ungrateful," she'd said, "but are you *sure* I'm the best qualified candidate you've seen?"

"You're the only candidate we've seen," replied Fred, the centre manager. "The only applicant, in fact. But that doesn't mean we're not *very* impressed. Perhaps we could even get a nice picture of you doing the Upside Down Dog to put on the advert?"

Since then, people had apparently been phoning up reception on a daily basis. The class was fully subscribed. Most of the students were local mothers, who wanted to come for yoga while their children were in playgroup next door. Lilli had spent all week devising a simple lesson for beginners. In all honesty she wasn't much more advanced herself. It would be a case of continuously keeping one step ahead — and hoping nobody in the class had a clue about yoga.

A good ice-breaker, she'd decided, would be the Roaring Lion. A great way to start off her class. Show them the fun side of her personality. Lilli stretched her thighs out and cracked her knuckles. Might as well limber up.

She knelt on the mat and crossed the front of her right ankle over the back of her left. The soles of her feet pointed out to the sides. She sat back so her buttocks snuggled down onto the heel of her right foot.

Her palms pressed firmly against tracksuited kneecaps, with fanned palms and fingers splayed out like the claws of a big cat.

She took a deep breath of air through the nose, and simultaneously opened her mouth very wide. Then her tongue stretched out as far as she could manage, curling down towards the chin. In the long mirror, Lilli could see herself looking more and more absurd with every movement. She bulged her eyes and contracted the muscles in her throat. Finally, she exhaled with a long, gentle growl. She could only imagine the merriment this display would spread amongst her students.

On the second inhalation, Lilli stared at the tip of her nose while she widened her mouth further and stuck out her tongue to the point of agony. She could see her cross-eyed reflection in the mirror, tongue lolling out, mouth stretched like a cavern. Completely ridiculous. But the class would love it. They would love *her*.

On the third and final inhalation, Lilli was paralyzed. As her lungs contracted and expanded with oxygen, something triggered in her nervous system. Her limbs stiffened and her face was stuck solid. She tried to roll to the side but it was no good. Her body was unresponsive. Even her eyeballs remained focused on the tip of her nose. A red spot was boiling up on it. She tried to cry out for help. But all that came out was a deep, leonine roar.

When the class arrived at half past nine, their new instructor was kneeling with her back to them, staring at herself in the mirror. Saliva was gathering on the tip of her tongue and there was a sticky wet patch on her lap. The students gathered around. She was breathing slowly, gruffly, and her body was rigid as marble.

Chantelle, one of the students, bent to look into Lilli's wonky eyes. "Excuse me, dear? Are you *alright*?"

Lilli purred.

"I know what's going on here," said Chantelle. "She's *meditating*. Completely *hypnotized*. Doesn't even know we're *here*."

Some of the class began to complain.

"No, you don't *understand*. She's leading by *example*. It's *inspirational*." Chantelle laid her tracksuit jacket on the floor, and carefully arranged herself in imitation of Lilli's posture, complete with protruding tongue, squinty stare and gentle growl.

"Well *come on*, you lot! Don't just *stand* there!"

Gradually they began copying Chantelle copying Lilli. Soon they were all balanced on their knees, droning contentedly. A stranger walking through the door into the yoga class would think nothing was out of place at all.

At half past ten, the mothers obediently stood and cracked their joints. They marvelled at Lilli's discipline, rigidity and self-control. As they trooped out the door, they whispered amongst themselves.

"She still hasn't budged an inch!"

"Isn't it mind-boggling?"

"What an odd-looking girl."

Soon the room was empty, apart from Lilli and Chantelle. The instructor still knelt, mouth gaping, tongue dangling out. Chantelle sighed and inspected Lilli from all angles. She walked around her, examined the shape of her body, the angles of her arms and legs, the expression of utter lunacy on her face. A thought came into Chantelle's mind. She closed the door and made a whispered telephone call.

Later that day a transit van was seen sitting outside the fire exit of the community centre, engine running, rear doors lying open. The driver didn't pay for a ticket, and was mounted up on the kerb; but he was only parked there for five minutes, so let's not get too judgmental. Anyone watching would have found the scene rather banal, apart from the brief moment when two burly men in black suits emerged from the fire exit. They carried between them a solid lump wrapped up in a blanket, and carefully loaded it into the van.

The Modern Art Gallery's new exhibit appeared without fanfare or hoopla or even a pamphlet. One day it wasn't there, the next day it was. Excitement for the new installation quickly spread, and people travelled from all over the city to gaze upon the display of post-modernist wrath and conservationist satire.

People laughed; people cried.

In the afternoon a group of tourists gathered to mimic the exhibit, dozens of them kneeling on the floor of the gallery. This earned Lilli Crabtree a plum front-page photograph in the local newspaper. All the readers and art-critics were in agreement; the Roaring Lion exhibit was a mystifying success.

Before long, documentary makers and freelance journalists were harassing the museum's management for more *intimate* access. After a long lunchtime of bartering, a deal was struck. Lilli was to be filmed, interrogated, and measured so that a waxwork model could be made. On the Saturday night, five days after the unfortunate paralysis, Lilli starred in her own prime time television program. The general public were whipped into an addicted froth and invited to dial premium rate telephone numbers to cast their vote on Lilli's fate. There were four options: permanent installation in the British Museum; delivery to China in exchange for political prisoners; placed on a plinth in a weather-proof bubble; or the television presenters could jimmy her jaw open and force-feed her grubs and bumblebees.

The voting was fierce. People discussed the topic on online messageboards, blogsites and transatlantic video calls. Everyone had an opinion. They were all voiced. Nobody listened to any besides their own.

In the end, it was the biggest scandal in the media that week. *Even though* the public had voted (in their millions), and *even though* they had dutifully telephoned (within the allotted timespan), and *even though* each of these calls cost one pound fifty (depending on the network), a rich philanthropist took Lilli's plight to heart and stepped in at the final moment. This man was called Benjamin Riddle, and he purchased Lilli's lease from the television company, who claimed to be subletting her from the museum, who seemed to have misplaced their receipt but confirmed ownership regardless. And so, finally, the poor yoga instructor was spared further public humiliation.

Benjamin operated an exclusive private clinic dedicated to the study, research, care and treatment for those suffering permanent paralysis. Lilli was promised sunlight, sustenance, dignity and frequent sessions with a feather duster.

Today, her fame has diminished, but she lives a much happier life. Occasionally Benjamin Riddle is charitable enough to open up the doors of his estate so the public can view his remarkable collection. She is not easy to find, but Lilli is there, surrounded by fellow patients, shaded from natural sunlight by a jungle of plastic trees. The whiskers implanted on both sides of her roaring mouth are, of course, artificial.

Meg Gannon

Click

Each day is different and changing,
and on this uneventful morning,
to save the inimitable now,
I raise my camera, creating pictures
as an evocation of how it is.

Click: In the morning haze distant mountains fold, blue-grey,
one against another, sheltering under a low-slung sky.

Click: The hebe bush sways in the cool breeze,
alive with carousing bees hovering.

Click: Canada geese rise to the sky, an arrow of intent,
aiming long necks as their broad wings beat.

Click: The fleet-footed sheep follow well-worn paths,
and stare distantly at me as I walk to the beach.

Click: An open boat rests on the shore, looped by an indolent rope,
waiting at slack water for the tug of the tide.

Click: Incoming, the restless sea rolls over stones,
washes the sand, swirling, shape-shifting,

and I know that as the years pass
the contours of the coast will be slowly redrawn
by the sea's insistent movement.

Meg Gannon

River

River, you have a mind of your own.
Gone is your slow sinuous slide. Today
you are no longer serene

but in spate. Turbulent water
steals colour from the earth
and your lyrical voice is lost.

Heedless,
splashing wildly
you cut through the valley
speeding over stones
hurtling in a rash descent

until, with the vitality of youth
eager for freedom
you leap,

tumbling
with the ease of an acrobat,
fearlessly.

Leela Soma

Dreams

A reef of dreams like a strand of pearls
dreams of a coral moon hanging low
on a sandy beach, the sea whispering secrets
our glances our eyes the only tongue, mesmerising
the rivers in me rise and flow like a crescendo
your touch as my body enfolds, you glow luciferous
my hopes shimmer in the pale moonlight, no
lodestar to guide me, I submit

life's

impermanence

etched on

the sand and salt

the receding waves

a dream

relived in

sandalwood scented nights

Leela Soma

Scrapbook

A scrapbook memory of breath and heartbeats
school summer break lovingly creating pages
colourful with words, images, drawings, dried
flowers, leaves, attempting poems words that
chime in alliteration, looking up dictionaries
swirling the words in the mouth, delicious like
ripe mango flesh bursting on the tongue
navigating happy days of childhood captured
in photos recorded on Brownie cameras, stuck
on buff vellum photo albums, white sticky edges
pasted with love and dreaming of a bright future.

Leela Soma

Laundrette

The peeling paint, the dirty roughcast on the walls outside
glaring deprivation marked *Temple Laundrette.* A face in the window
made me glance again. Wan, carrying the weight of the world on her
shoulders, she looked out and our eyes met for a second.

Years spun away like the huge churning machine grey clothes spinning,
a young immigrant with no place in a tiny flat
with no washing machine carrying the bag of unwashed laundry
to a dark place like this one, was it the *West End Laundrette*?

Worrying for the right change in her hands holding new unfamiliar money
watched in despair as the homesickness rose in her like the soapy foam
in the machine, cleansing away the old and folding in the new.
She turned away.
I did the same.

Jean Taylor

Rime

The salt-wife's days are filled
with the business of sea-harvesting,
of lugging buckets of brine from
the shore's edge to the pans.

She knows that the water will form
into air, that salt will begin to sparkle.
She imagines the glitter of ballrooms,
the caper of highland reels.

Her clothing is salt-caked, her hands
cracked and stinging — a chill fret
stiffens her cheeks. She is urgent
to leave, toe-tapping impatient.

She would soar with the sea mews
to seek out a lover, to feel his fingers
slide a slow vibrato
along the stretch of her back,

shiver as he stroked the pale silk
of her slip over the curve of her belly
as he bent towards her —
lips grazing on lips.

But the wind swoops through winter
branches. The sky is snow white
above a sea of feathers. Inside her,
black ice hardens.

Federation of Writers (Scotland) 2019 Vernal Equinox Competition

Prizewinners

Flash Fiction:	1	Colin Kerr
	2	Bert Thomson
	3	Steve May
Gaelic Poetry:	1	Deborah Moffatt
	2	Sgàire Uallas
	HC	Peter Clive [1]
Short Story:	1	Montague Chambers
	2	Steve May
	3	William Sutton
Poetry:	1	Mary Wight
	2	Elaine Webster
	3	Jilly O'Brien

Judges:

Flash fiction:	Gordon Lawrie
Gaelic poetry:	Marcas Mac an Tuairneir
Short stories:	Olga Wojtas
Poetry:	Stephen Watt

---

[1] A Highly Commended poem is included because of the low number of Gaelic entries.

Steve May

What good's a cowboy?

War-cries. Galloping hooves up the alleyway. Garden gate slammed open wide. Teddy boy, like on telly. Snatches me hat off; laughs, sneers *Where's yer mummy then?*

She appears. He sniggers. She tries to grab back the hat; he just laughs, throws her down, shoots off.

My Lone Ranger cowboy hat; black felt, with red and white tassels. Chaps to go with it. Holster and gun. But no good without the hat; you had to have that to be a real cowboy.

Don't worry he's gone now, she said. *We'll get you another one.*

I cried.

But, mum, why couldn't you get it off him?

Inside for cuddles; tighter, but less secure than before.

Vernal Equinox Competition: Flash Fiction: Third Prize

Bert Thomson

Daft and Dafter

"Here's what happened.

"When ah woke up this morning, ah wis rattlin like a Sally Army tambourine, so ah went doon tae the Barnardo's shop in Shawlands. Ah wis gonny knock something an sell it so ah could score a tenner bag, but there wis some folk in the shop when ah went in.

"That's when ah saw Jason, staunin in the middle ay the shop wae a wean in a buggy.

"Well ah knew Jason hud a motor, an ah knew a guy in Largs that wid let me have some gear on tick, so ah asks Jason if he could gie me a run tae Largs an he says aye.

"So as we're leaving ah goes, 'Ah'll get the wean,' an ah pushed the buggy oot the door efter him.

"Over at his car, the first thing ah says is, 'Where's the baby seat?' an Jason goes, 'Ah bumped that years ago.' So ah jist strapped the wean inty the back seat.

"Doon at Largs, the guy sorted us oot an we decided to take some ay the gear there and then. Then the guy's missus came in an said she wid take the wean tae Nardini's fur a cone an gie it a shot ay the wee cars doon at the front.

"They came back aboot an oor later, an me Jason an the wean went back tae Glesca. Jason hud tae get his wee boy fae the school in Shawlands at three.

"So we picked the wee man up an we'd barely turned the corner roon fae the school when your mob appeared, pointin guns at us an shoutin, 'Get oot the car.'

"You keep talkin aboot abduction, but it's Jason's wean. He wis staunin right next tae it in the shop."

Scrimgeour stared at Wilson.

"You see Ryan, the trouble wae that story is, that we've got Jason through the room and he's saying it's your wean."

"Ma wean? Whit wid ah wahnt a wean fur? It's no ma wean, Charlie."

"Naw, ah know it's no your wean. An it's no Jason's wean either. It belongs tae a lassie that wis in the shop," said Scrimgeour.

"Aw well, nae herm done, eh? The wean hud a great time."

"Nae herm done?" Scrimgeour was shouting. "The wean had a great time? I've had a terrified lassie to deal with. I've had a police helicopter in the air for hours. I've had every cop in Glasgow looking for that kid all day, while you two, Daft" — he pointed at Wilson — "and even Dafter through the room there, have had a day at the fucking seaside."

He looked at his watch.

"This is Detective Inspector Charles Scrimgeour. It's twenty-one twenty-three hours on Thursday the sixteenth of August, twenty-eighteen. I'm temporarily stopping this recorded interview with Ryan Wilson to allow me to confer with colleagues."

Scrimgeour pressed the off switch and stood up to leave.

Wilson looked up hopefully. "Any chance ay a fag, big man? Ah'm Choke-ahontas here."

Vernal Equinox Competition: Flash Fiction: Second Prize

Colin Kerr

Charlotte

Near the end, we dragged the piano out the door and left it in the street.

I moved here from a village you wouldn't know. I moved here to be with Charlotte. We never meant to stay here long but time passes. The leak in the skylight grew, stains expanded and the carpets lost their appeal. The furniture evolved from quaint to irritating to looming monuments to inertia. Time changes everything. Dust becomes sticky and keys go untouched.

Charlotte was one of those people who'd claim whatever she could. The party, the rules of a game or someone else's illness. You name it, she'd been there, had had it worse or knew someone who had.

I'd met Charlotte just four months before. She was on the street holding a placard. Resting it on the ground. A protestor waiting for a cause.

"Gods in the sky," it read.

"A film? A band?" I asked.

"Gods in the sky," she said as she waved it generally above her.

"Gods in the sky."

An hour later we were on a train to Wrexham, the sign in a bin. She looked cold. I'd have offered her a blanket if I'd had one. Moving in together was inevitable. Some changes are choices but with Charlotte, there was inevitability.

"Look. A piano," she said when we viewed the house. "Do you know how to play?" she squirmed, squeezing my arm.

I became convinced the piano was haunted. I became convinced the whole place was haunted. It oppressed. It seeped. Then it corroded.

Accents were another thing Charlotte would appropriate. She'd change like a shadow in the wind. We'd be standing in a queue, returning last week's hope, next thing her voice would become the assistant's voice. Generally people would ignore her but occasionally a look would appear across the counter. Maybe we all change, adapt to blend in. I've been mistaken for someone's missing relative. Standing outside a charity shop with a bag of self-help books, an expectant voice called me. For a split second, I wondered whether I was their missing relative, my name always seemed lacking.

That Saturday we were looking at cushions. I was tired of cushions. Tired of wandering from shop to shop comparing soft furnishings. We bought no cushions. We bought another vase and I agreed to give consideration to knitting classes. It was one new thing after another. Hopes. Solutions.

"Just leave it," I whispered. "Come on. Get up, it's over." Charlotte was kneeling in the rain, exhausted. Kneeling there, sobbing, stroking a leg of the piano. It sat there for three days. Rained on, sniffed and claimed by dogs and played on by kids. Eventually someone came and took it away. I was out when that happened. Or maybe something else happened. All I know is one day, it was gone. That happens. Something is here, then something is gone.

Vernal Equinox Competition: Flash Fiction: First Prize

Peter Clive

Figheachan

Théid a' h-uile figheachan ás,
is crìonidh lus-chrùin air falbh.

Bha iomadh pioramaid aig Phàraoh,
a dh'aindeoin a bhith gach meud aca
deagh-thomhaiste mar fhada cus,
direach taigh ro chaol mu dheireadh.

Anns a' chiad uaigh chladhaich sinne
funnd gach uile bailtean móra daonnachd.
Chur a' chlach-chinn aice an stéidh ruinn
is cuiridh sinn ar eachdraidh sìos oirre
nuair a tha ar làithean a' dol gu luath
agus a tha feum orra ath-lìonadh

oir chan eil a' shìobhaltachd ach bròn
an déidh am bàs a' chiad dhuine,
is tha a' h-uile fàglaich earras-uaighe
leis an do dhùisg an talamh.

Vernal Equinox Competition: Gaelic Poetry: Highly Commended

English translation

Wreath

All wreaths will fade away
and garlands wither.

Pharaoh's many pyramids,
despite their every dimension
being well-reckoned as excessive,
were just too narrow in the end.

In the first grave we dug the founds
of each and every city of Humanity.
Its headstone is our foundation stone,
and we will lay history upon it
while our days still turn to dust
and are in need of replenishment,

for civilisation is but sorrow
after the death of the first man
and all that remains is grave goods
with which the earth was awoken.

Sgàire Uallas

Marbhrann MhicCodruim dheireannaich

Bu dùmhail dlùth na cagraichean
an latha rinn thu caochladh;
na cabagan cumanta
a' sanas ann am faclan air thuar bhith truasail
am faochaidh a bhith cuidhte 's
truaill-chuimhne do thràill-ghineil.

Ghabh iad do bhloigh-bheannachd
gu saoirsneil
amhail mar a ghabh iad bho shean
làn-bhuaidhean do dhream;
buaidh na nàire
's i buaidh na h-àilleachd
is buaidh na bàrdachd:
buaidhean mnà-mhara ghil 's i cuarta
air cridheachan dust is luatha.

Ach is cinnteach
gur buan a fhuaradh thu,
's nach robh ann ad chaochladh
ach iomlaid chochall;
gun do leig thu dhìot do bhian daonna
's gun d' fhuair d' anam-mara
air èirigh às an aitreabh-èislein
gud phrìomh-mhàthair 's i cruinn led chàirdean
nam mìle sùil sgàthandubh
a' plubadaich bàidh mu bharra-thuinn,
is fodhpa gad dhùileachadh
nad dhùthaich bhuntainnich fhèin.

Mar a chunnaic muinntir ur gin-èigneachaidh
ur mì-fhreumhachaidh
ur sìor-cheusaidh;
's gun do ghabh iad ìoghnadh.

Vernal Equinox Competition: Gaelic Poetry: Second Prize

English translation by Nathaniel Harrington

Death-Verse for the last MacCodrum

The whispers were close, crowding
on the day you passed,
the common gossips
saying all the right words to sound compassionate
relieved to be rid of you and
the contaminated memory of your thrall-lineage.

They accepted your half-farewell
freely
just as they had long accepted
all the gifts of your kin;
an effect of shame
is the gift of beauty
and the gift of poetry:
the gifts of a white sea-woman, tormented
by hearts of dust and ash.

But it is certain
that you weathered everything,
and that your passing was only
an exchange of shells;
that you set aside your human hide
and that your sea-soul managed
to rise out of the dwelling of grief
towards your first mother, where your friends gathered,
a thousand mirror-black eyes
splashing kindness over the wave-tops,
and under them, expecting you
in your own country of belonging.

While those who raped your kin
                                        uprooted you
                                        crucified you
saw
and were amazed.

Deborah Moffatt

Beatha ùr

Moch sa mhadainn chithinn i
a' coiseachd sìos gu iomall a' chladaich,
a brù torrach, a cìochan lìontach,
a ceum rèidh.

Àm a' chuir a bh' ann,
na fir anns na h-achaidhean
leth-chaillte ann an neul duslaich,
an talamh a' dùsgadh fon casan,

mise nam sheasamh aig an uinneig,
a' coimhead air na tuinn luasganach,
stoirm de dh'fhaclan 's ìomhaighean
a' cathadh nam inntinn.

Mu àm na buana, chunnacas i
a' coiseachd le pram, a leanabh òg
paisgte ann am plaide, buinn airgid
a' deàrrsadh air a' chluasaig.

Aig deireadh an fhoghair
bidh na fir anns an taigh-seinnse
ag òl air a chèile gu beul an latha,
uisge-beatha a' dortadh thar an làir,

mise an seo, mo chùl ris an uinneig,
faclan a' sruthadh thar na duilleige,
beatha ùr, slàn, a' tighinn gu bith
à talamh torrach m' inntinne.

Vernal Equinox Competition: Gaelic Poetry: First Prize

English translation

New life

Early in the morning I would see her
walking to the edge of the shore,
her gait slow and easy, her breasts
swollen, her belly full.

It was planting time, the men
working in the fields, half-hidden
in a cloud of dust, the ground
awakening beneath their feet,

while I, standing at the window,
stared out over the restless sea,
a storm of words and images
drifting through my mind.

Near harvest time
she was seen with a pram,
her baby swaddled in a blanket,
silver coins shining on the pillow.

Come harvest home, the men
are in the pub at night,
spilling whisky on the floor,
toasting one another until dawn,

and here I am, my back to the window,
words streaming across the page,
a whole new world coming to life
out of the fertile ground of my mind.

Notes:
"torrach" in Gaelic means fertile, either as in pregnant or as in land.
"a' cathadh" means drifting (as of snow) and also "battling"

Jilly O'Brien

Now that I'm no longer dying

my husband has returned to his natural state of lukewarm dinner guest. He pats the dog, chair bound, cold shouldered skink padding to his rock in muddy shoes via black kitchen tiles and no plate although his sandwich is pretty much a loaf of tomorrow's lunchboxes. Through the crumbs, there are vague child enquiries and flickering sideways glances at the washing machine. Now that I'm no longer dying, no longer lying awake at three a.m. humming

la la la la can't hear you can't hear you can't hear you lie still even stiller than that and they won't know it's you

at thoughts pressing hard from all sides on a deep ocean dive to stop me breathing until my eardrums burst, I've put my ear plugs back in. My sister did that once when we were six and eight, a sleeping bag race to the bottom and back, only I was tricked when she sat on the only way out

and she was older and I wasn't strong enough it's too hot I can't breathe lie still lie even stiller than that and she'll let you out

Four weeks of limbo sore in a floral gown, machines out-of-date magazines needles biopsies careful sympathy and staring at the ceiling, now that I'm no longer dying, my husband has returned to his natural state of general irritability and his unwavering faith that a clean shirt will appear

in the morning.

Vernal Equinox Competition: Poetry: Third Prize

Elaine Webster

Living the language

Swimming and breathing, new-borns in water
soaking up stories through pale perfect skin
mothers talk to them, catch the word-droplets
teens turning from them to dive darkly in

down to the crannies scorned by the timid
ripple with accents and guttural stops
howk after phrases spat in smug faces
slather in swashes of black badderlocks

grannies stay shtum, not sure what they're feeling
steep aching feet in the waves of verb-lists
knotted kind fingers, picking and sorting
cradle the rare phrase to place in the kist

shingle is noisy, strangers come listen
scoop salted lyrics all eager to sing
clapping at couplets to take to the city
beating out rhythms from razorbill wings

writhing in rhythm, teens keen to follow
switching to Scots, seeking sinewy sounds
bletherin gaitherin, wirkin thigither
banterin haiverin hunkerin roond

plowterin pleiterin, aw clartit in saund
slaisterin pleisterin, wird-watter soused
leid licht an sonsie, jist as it stertit
sweemin an braithin, caller, an lowsed.

Vernal Equinox Competition: Poetry: Second Prize

Mary Wight

Fish

Coins of molten sun
dripped slow into the river's mouth,
heat yet to go when three women
arrived, neither young nor old,
a sudden, sparkling wave of whitest gold.

Cider ordered, handbags and haunches
settled, elbows rested on weathered wood.
Laughter rose in gusts, seemed to alter
the very density of the air,
everything pulled to a point.

This team had spent their day
cleaning rented rooms, changing sheets,
wiping down, and now, all doing over,
reward: a sliver of time theirs to savour.

Talk was of tomorrow's
roll-over lottery, holidays
to book if they won, grandkids to treat.
Meantime new sandals, this weather
and oh, how good it was.

A Jim was mentioned, whether
son, husband, or other, unclear but
the woman's voice rounded in pride.
He'd sailed before dawn. There would be
fish on their table tonight.

I gulped dregs, fingers white on glass
held too tight, ash and blackened weeds
fell, left me suddenly ravenous,
ravenous for a man I would never know,
his dark-skied promise of fish.

Vernal Equinox Competition: Poetry: First Prize

William Sutton

Guilt written

His email bleeped. He had notifications turned off, normally, but he was expecting a message from the magazine editor.

> SHORT STORY: HARD-BOILED, LIGHT-HEARTED.
> DEADLINE: 11 JUNE.
> PLEASE NOTE REVISED FEE.*

Dougie O'Dowd (nom de plume) fired off his customary email, accepting. He smoothed his notebook, eager to get writing. This was his time to get the words down. He wouldn't let intrusions snarl up his ideas. As he went to open a new document, his eyes were sucked back to the email message. To that asterisk.

"Revised fee." He scrolled down, muttering. "Fee, fee, fee..."

Hidden beneath the disclaimers lurked the attachment. He stabbed at the mouse. NewSchedule.pdf opened brazenly over the email:

> IN LINE WITH THE MAGAZINE'S FINANCIAL STRICTURES, WE HAVE REVISED OUR PAYMENT SCHEDULE.

The blow was delivered carelessly. He rubbed his eyes.

> SHORT FICTION, 1500 WORDS: £50.

Dougie gripped the screen. If it had been a piece of paper, he would have scrumpled it up. He heard the strange inhuman wail before he realised he was making it. He released his grip, colours flaring where his thumbs had pressed the screen. He stood up, banged his head, sat down. The tantrum flared.

"All right, dear?" called his wife, Eileen, from down in the kids' room. Eileen didn't know about his tantrums. Maybe she suspected, from little things his former colleagues had said.

"Fine." He gripped his desk, and breathed. He thought of his therapist: we build walls, to protect our inner selves. When those walls are vulnerable, little things burst through. "Fine!"

Stories were Dougie's new milieu. He had done well to find a print magazine that accepted a story every month; he worked hard to keep them happy — and their readers.

"Fifty quid," he muttered. "Wodehouse got double that in 1905. I got double that last week."

A story of fifteen hundred words took a week to write. The germ of an idea; snatches of dialogue; long walks; draft; rewrites. His writing group mauling it; his wife red-lining it. Word count. Spellcheck. Submit, in despair.

Now this insult.

"What's up, dear?" Eileen called.

His credit card was shredded. His overdraft was overstretched. He shouldn't have suggested a holiday. Dougie O'Dowd felt a benevolent gaze upon him.

"NO MATTER." Samuel Beckett pierced him with gull-like eyes. "FAIL AGAIN. FAIL BETTER."

Alongside Beckett, on his wall of heroes, Andy McNab stood at ease: "KEEP WORKING."

"PUT ONE WORD AFTER ANOTHER," Neil Gaiman chipped in, "UNTIL YOU HAVE A BOOK."

"INSPIRATION," Johnny Marr declared, "MUST FIND YOU WORKING."

Bastard magazine. Plunging him below minimum wage. Fifty quid? Better than nothing, though. If he kept the fifty pounds clear of the overdraft, he could take the family to Arran. Another story would get a campsite...

One step at a time.

He rubbed his old police badge, for luck, as he always did, before putting words on paper. He began typing, doggedly, word on word.

> Mikey O'Mara walked into the editor's office. Without saying a word, he affixed the silencer to his Smith and Wesson pistol. The editor had not looked up. Yet.

Dougie O'Dowd sat back, struggling to fight off a smile.

> Mikey cleared his throat.
>
> Rosanna the editor looked up. She registered the weapon with the weary look of an employer who has stared too long down the barrel of a gun. She almost

welcomed it. After he shot her, Mikey walked out with the cash box. No jangling, all bank notes. Nobody stopped him; they knew he was to be fired. Nobody challenged him; they felt sorry for him.

Control S. Save document. Title? Employee Harassment.

Strong start, yes, but was it credible? His stupid protagonist would get caught long before the 1500-word mark. Control Z: undo, undo, undo.

Mikey O'Mara asked politely if he might see the editor. The secretary didn't recognise him. Glasses from a charity shop (only 50 pence); add in shaved head, stoop, and limp, and even the editor didn't recognise Mikey. Just as well; otherwise she'd have fired him.

Sadly, for her, he fired first.

Dougie O'Dowd raised his eyebrow at this verbal flourish. His ex-copper's brain kicked in: no, no, no. Mikey needed to be smarter. He should get the editor to hand over the money, so he'd touched nothing. Better still, make her transfer the money to an untraceable account, then leave her tied up, but alive, so suspicion fell upon her.

This was the moment he always loved in the drafting process, where he knew he had something. The details might be obscure, but he had the engine.

He scrolled up. Started rewriting. To channel his writer's wrath through his ex-copper's filter. Make it eye-wateringly convincing. Use those anomalies he'd noted in the force.

Change the editor to some other, more lucrative job: finance. He began writing apace, his brow glistering. Nobody would discern the idea's origin: the satisfaction of his revenge would glow brighter still.

Eileen came up mid-evening with his tea. He was confused.

"So soon?"

She pointed to the time in the corner of his screen, smiling.

"I lost track."

"How many words?" She laid the cup on his desk. On the saucer, the biscuit's chocolate was melting. She must have been waiting for him to pause.

It was their evening ritual. She got home from work, then took care of the kids. Dougie retreated up the stairs to write. 'The siege in the room,' Beckett called his glory years, stuck at his desk for days on end, writing his masterpieces. Dougie might only manage six till nine p.m., but every night felt like a siege to him. By nine-thirty the kids were asleep, but they'd wake him at dawn; so they never sat up long together before bedtime.

Dougie tapped Control P. "I've no idea." He stared at the pages streaming from the laser printer, struggling to connect them with his labours.

She squeezed his shoulder. He was lucky she was supportive. The others in his writing group were divorced; they could start a jewellers' with the rings. She pointed at the screen: 4612 words.

"Bloody hell." He thumped his fist on the desk. A drop of tea splashed on to the screen.

Eileen dabbed at it with a tissue, tensed. "What now?"

"I'll have to cut it to shreds." He clenched his teeth. "Meet the word count."

"Too many words? Hardly something to complain about." She lifted the pages out of his reach. "Let me read it."

She was totally absorbed. He never usually let her read the first draft, or the second. He waited till it was polished, ready to go; then she'd glance through it on the sofa, TV blaring, underlining odd phrases, and tell him it was fine. Now she was sitting, mouth open, turning the pages on her lap, TV on mute.

He held his breath.

She laid down the red pen, absently turning the telly off. "Another story there," she muttered, turning to the last page.

Another story? He opened his mouth, but didn't want to interrupt her reading. Maybe he had written a multi-part narrative. Which meant he could split it up. Which meant he'd written not just this story but the following month's too.

She re-read the final paragraph, with its vengeful twist. She put down the final page, looking at him, eyes bright. "These are the best stories you've ever written."

He blinked rapidly. "I just imagined what it would be like. To do the crimes."

"To do the crimes." Her shining eyes showed she was imagining it too. "And when they're closing in on him, on the last page, and we're rooting for him, despite everything, and we're sure they've got him. Then we realise he's tricked them all and laid the trail to the manager's door, so that she's going to get punished for everything he's done —"

"That's a good moment?"

She gazed through the skylight, as if it were their glowing future. "A great moment."

He seized the chance to mention the money. He hated to moan, but it seemed so unfair, to halve his fee.

Eileen refused to be dismayed. "You're getting paid for writing. Besides, this isn't just one story."

He swallowed. "Cut it in two?"

"Two? Screw your courage to the sticking place. There's ideas enough in there for ten stories. And so realistic: you could use them as the blueprint to carry out the actual crimes."

He glanced over at his police badge. "That would pay better."

She jogged his shoulder, her eyes full of amusement. Snuggling up against him, Eileen smiled, thinking through the crimes so beautifully detailed in his stories.

The magazine's popularity soared. The first story, *Employer Harassment*, introduced his anti-hero Mikey O'Mara — no longer a magazine writer, but a hedge fund employee with a vendetta against his manager.

The readers cried out for more. As the stories grew more sophisticated, so did O'Mara's methods. The rate for short fiction remained the same. But Dougie did get enquiries from other magazines, then agents, and finally publishers.

All That Glisters was a jewellery theft.

Me Myself and Identity was a hyper-modern fraud story on an international scale.

Things got darker with *Crosstown Trafficking*. He included authentic details: the police servers blocking vulnerable witnesses' verbatim testimony, as it was full of filthy language; the cuddly pig the police took to obligatory counselling after a raid. "How do I feel about what I saw? Let's ask Piggy here."

Phisherman's Blues was a rollicking yarn of ex-money man O'Mara using his knowledge to carry out the phishing frauds he used to foil. The back story hinted that O'Mara stole from the rich to benefit the poor.

His wife loved the stories. When he'd left the police force, stressed and exhausted, she'd listened to his woes and supported him. When his therapist suggested writing down his experiences to shake off depression, she'd encouraged him. They could survive on her salary. He took care of the kids. They made time for him to write. It wasn't work like before, but he kept strict hours, improving his craft. He soon started submitting work. He sold bits and pieces, until this magazine began accepting monthly stories. He was contributing, at least. Now with his book deal alongside Eileen's unexpected bonuses, their money problems were evaporating.

With the magazine's popularity, though, it was inevitable someone would notice the correlation.

In the month that any given story appeared, a copycat crime would take place. Each month a new plot, each month a new crime. Eileen followed the newspaper reports with interest; Dougie paid them little heed. The police initially thought it was a smart-arsed reader, jumping on the plotlines as a weird homage. But the timing was too tight: the crimes must be planned before the magazine came out.

Suspicion fell on the publishing house. Computers were seized, paperwork inspected. The only person who had worked on all the stories was the editor. She was arrested, suspected of colluding with the crimes, if not instigating them. The charges didn't stick. But she lost her job, just as the Mikey O'Mara series came to an end. She didn't recommend Dougie to the incoming editor.

Dougie O'Dowd didn't mind. He was taking a break from writing.

They lazed by the Jacuzzi in the Isle of Arran hotel, the kids happy in the complimentary crèche. His wife was reading through the last story in the magazine, resting on her Egyptian cotton bathrobe. She turned the page back and forth, as if she'd missed something.

He looked at her. "You're disappointed."

She shrugged. "I was waiting for the bit when we realise he's laid the clues to the door of the manager who stitched him up. I loved that bit, where we realise it's all been his elaborate revenge."

"Too obvious. Police would see through it." Dougie sipped at his drink. "I rewrote it. To make it more credible."

Short Story Third Prize

Steve May

The man in the corner

A man wept into a bar. He didn't get a drink, just went straight to a table in the corner and slumped, head in hands. Everyone looked at him when he came in and their eyes followed him to the table, stayed there for a few seconds, then turned back to their drinks and conversations. You could hear him sobbing through the dull thud of the piped music, not because his crying was loud, but because you rarely heard that kind of thing. A man crying in a bar.

He wept into his hands. His hands must have been pretty wet by now. Sometimes he'd stop, look up, then start again with renewed force, more desperate, almost howling. He appeared inconsolable, though no one tried to console him. There were a few people in the bar who could have tried, but they chose not to. Or maybe it never crossed their minds.

The barman had never encountered this sort of thing before. He wondered whether to ask him if he wanted a drink, but thought better of it.

Most people in this man's situation would go home to cry. Perhaps he didn't have a home to cry in. But he looked smartly dressed, as if he'd come from a day at the office. His tie was loosened, that was all, but you often got that when men finished work. And his hands were soiled. Perhaps he'd had a bad day at the office. Perhaps his wife had gone off with the postman or something. Perhaps his dog had died. These are the kind of things that might make you sit in a bar and weep. But there was no telling what might have happened; he definitely wasn't telling; not that anybody asked.

Closing time drew near and the room started to clear. It's amazing that people hadn't left before then, having to put up with a man crying, albeit in a corner. You'd think it would have spoiled their drink, soured their evening a little, at least made them sad or even depressed. But it seemed not.

When the barman rang his bell and called out time gentlemen please, it was ironic because there was only one man left in the pub and he certainly wasn't behaving like a gentleman; he was crying. He didn't respond. And when the barman said finish your drinks off please, he didn't respond to that either, because he hadn't got a drink to finish.

It wasn't usually too bad being a barman. He picked up all the empty glasses, then went round again and put the chairs on top of the tables. His nightly routine. He worked his way around the man still sitting at his table sobbing. He put no chairs on that one; he couldn't anyway, because the man's head still lay on it. But he wasn't too careful with the others; in fact, he made as much noise as possible. After all, he had to let the man know it was time to go. Still, he didn't move.

He turned the main pub lights off, leaving on only the one above the bar. The sound of the man weeping seemed quite eerie now, with no music to distract from it. Merely the faintest whimper in the closed down dimly-lit bar. The man wept into himself. He must have had a lot of space inside to hold all these tears. Surprising he had any tears left.

What could the barman do? He reminded the man of the time; no reaction. He tried to lift him from his seat, but his body just became more rigid, as if frozen to the spot. What then? It would be silly to call the police; crying might be irritating, but it wasn't a crime. Should he call an ambulance? Well, the man still had plenty of strength, judging by the way he'd repelled all his attempts to lift him.

So he left him there to cry out the night. Perhaps he'd be OK in the morning. Perhaps he just needed a good night's cry.

In the morning, the cleaner came in. It wasn't a hard job being a cleaner in this pub; rarely did anyone spew on the floor or anything, not even in the bogs. She had her routine and the job more or less did itself once she got started. Soon the pub would be wiped clean, ready for the lunchtime rush.

She began to notice a strange odour. Even though she was used to sniffing things in her job, she couldn't put her finger on this one. It led her to the far corner, to a table with no chairs stacked on it. On the floor was a deep pool. When she bent down to smell it, she became engulfed with nausea. It was salty, but so intense and bitter it made her want to vomit. Like washed-up rotting seaweed. When she stood up, she felt dizzy, her head spinning. She had to sit down for a bit to recover, before mopping up the mess. She was worried that smell might be hard to get rid of.

Short Story Second Prize

Going home

January 3rd

I'm different from the other boys, I know I am. It's not just the way I look. Mum tells me I'm her handsome boy, but then she would, wouldn't she?

I'm back at home again. That makes 19 visits to the hospital, but only since I started counting. I have been ill, forever.

This is going to be my New Year diary, but I'm rubbish at diaries, so it will only be when I remember.

Since Dad left, Mum has been a lot better. She and I talk all the time now.

I have asked Mum about myself, but she says my sickness is "complicated." She looks funny when I ask things. There is something she isn't telling me, I know it. Adults do that a lot, like when Mum says, "Everything's fine," and then you hear her go away and start crying.

What is it about me that's different? Why does it make her cry?

January 4th

Hugo came round today. He's my best friend from School. He gets picked on by the bullies, a lot, just as I do. Mr Stainsgill told them off for saying unkind things but that only made it worse.

Hugo is into Sci-fi and cool things like that. He has crazy ideas which make me laugh. I like being at home, because he comes to see me.

After Hugo left, Mum came in looking upset. She had a bad phone call. She always looks like that after one.

She said I won't be going back to School any more. I think that's great, but I am a bit worried about Hugo. Without me there, the bullies will all pick on him.

Mum looked as though she was going to cry. I pointed at the window. The sun was shining in the garden. I told her you can't be sad when the sun is shining. Then she REALLY started crying. I don't understand grownups sometimes.

Back to hospital in a couple of weeks.

January 15th

There's a bird singing outside the window. I can hear it from my bed and I nearly saw it once or twice. It's been singing every day I have been in the hospital. I tried really hard, but I can't quite get round far enough to see where it is.

The Nurse caught me trying to look and told me off for nearly falling out of bed. I explained about the bird. She said it was just an old thrush and I shouldn't worry about it, because they're really common.

This one isn't common, though, because of all the thrushes in the world, it sings outside MY window. That makes it special. Why can't she see that?

January 18th

Mum told me today that I'm her "little star." She said that when my dad and she got together to make me as a baby, they saw a shooting star. They were in the playground at Longton Green. I know the one; I've been there.

I told Hugo, and he said that it must have been a UFO. People always say they're shooting stars, or meteors, because they're frightened of aliens. Could he be right? Could I be an alien, rescued from the crash of a flying saucer?

It would explain a lot of things. The trouble I have with breathing and being tired all the time. The atmosphere on my home planet could be quite different to Earth. Then there's the problem I have, with a lot of food making me chuck up. My body isn't used to Earth type food.

That's why the Doctors keep making me come back to the hospital, so they can study me. They must know...

January 26th

When Hugo came round today, he said that I might be from Mars. I told him that was silly, because everyone knows that the Solar System is devoid of life. It says so on Wikipedia.

I must be from a lot further away, like another star system. I suggested Arcturus and I think he was quite impressed. I didn't tell him that was the only one I knew the name of!

Hugo wanted to know if my people would come for me. He was trying to be nice, but really, I think he was excited by the idea of seeing aliens, like in Dr Who.

I thought about this after he went home. How would I contact them? People in films always have a rescue beacon device. If Mum was in Longton Green playground, when she saw the shooting star that was really a UFO, maybe there's something there. Something, left from the crash, I could use?

I could call my people, tell them I'm here, and need rescuing. Would they come?

February 10th

I saw the thrush at the hospital today! No one was in the room and it flew down on the window sill. I said hello to it, and it said hello back! It was awesome.

Then the stupid Nurse came in and frightened it off. I got very angry at her and she got all huffy and went away.

Mum came in, and told me off, and said I shouldn't shout at the Nurse. She was only trying to help. I tried to explain about the thrush, but she shut me up, and said I mustn't get excited, or I'd make myself more ill. So, I was quiet, and she said I was a good boy.

Why are adults so grumpy? It's great to have your own bird singing outside your window isn't it? I know it's not a phoenix, or anything grand, but it's still mine.

I hope that when I get to be as old as they are, I'm not grumpy like that!

February 14th

It's true. I AM an alien.

I heard the Doctors talking to Mum. They closed the door, but it swung open again a little, and I could hear bits of what they were saying.

The Doctor was talking about a test they'd done on me — I missed the name. Then he said, "He's not your child, is he?"

Mum started crying and then admitted it. "I have never told him where he came from," she said.

Well she wouldn't tell me I was an alien, would she? I'd run off to find my people and their planet, and then she'd be on her own. I think she likes having me around.

The Doctor also said something about my illness. They said that they expected the change to come soon and I should be monitored. Mum said she would watch me closely, so that she could tell them when it happened.

They never told me I would change into something! It's like a caterpillar becoming a butterfly. I must be going to change into whatever my proper alien form is. That's why Mum cries a lot. She likes having her own little boy, but when I change, what then?

Will I be big or small? Perhaps I'll leave my body behind, and just be pure energy, like those aliens on Star Trek. That's why they want to watch me. They'll want to do all kinds of experiments on me to find out what I am.

How do I stop them?

February 16th

I'm back at home now, because the Doctors said they couldn't do anything more for me. I guess they're waiting for the Change so they can start their experiments.

When Hugo came, I told him about what the doctors had said, and the big change that was coming. He got very excited, and wanted to know if I would have tentacles, and nine eyes.

I don't FEEL like I am going to have tentacles, but maybe wings. I wasn't that bothered about the eyes. He got really excited then, and shouted, "Wings would be so cool, bro! If you do, you have to come fly over my house. I'll take a video of it and we can put it on YouTube and Instagram! We'll make a mint of money!"

I had to wait for him to stop jumping about before going on. I wasn't sure that I wanted to be on the Internet as an alien. Wouldn't all the governments come to find me, to shoot me, and stop me invading?

Hugo assured me that the vid would make millions, but he was quite decent about it, and promised to go halves.

February 18th

Hugo came for the last time today.

My plans are made. I told Hugo before, that I was leaving, and he was very sad. When he was giving me the stuff I asked for, he said that he would miss me, and gave me a hug.

So, I said that he could have all my Star Wars stuff, even the signed photo that we got from the fundraising Mum did. I think that cheered him up a bit.

Grandpa told me that when people go away, they write wills which are legal things that say what stuff they are going to give people. It's the law.

I don't know any lawyers though, so I'll have to hope that someone finds this diary, and that they do the right thing by Hugo.

My Star Wars stuff is pretty good. I hope the adults don't steal it for themselves and not tell Hugo. Sometimes, they can be awfully mean.

February 21st

Well this is it. Not long to go, now. I am sorry I can't say goodbye to Mum properly, but she'd tell the Doctors, and then they'd call the army, and I'd be locked up somewhere like the Tower of London, or the White House.

I said I felt tired, so Mum tucked me in bed. Actually, I feel stronger than I ever have. She went off to the shops to get something nice for tea. That will take her at least an hour.

I'll give her ten minutes, then dress myself and slip out of the window. I am going to go to the Longton Green playground; it's not far. Hugo made me a map from the Internet.

There's still plenty of light outside. I'll go there when it's dark, find the beacon, and call my people. I've never been out by myself. It's time to complete my mission and explore this new, alien world.

Excerpt from the Rawton Evening Herald February 24th

We can confirm, sadly, that the body recovered on Friday night from Longton Green Playground, is that of Charlie Jones, the previously reported missing boy.

Police officers said that he was found next to the playground's well-known central feature, which looks like a flying saucer. His mother said that he had loved that feature as a toddler.

Speaking to reporters, Mrs Barbara Jones, 41, thanked the monumental effort made by the community to help find her missing child. She told the Herald that her son had a serious condition with medical complications, and this had meant many visits to hospital. She believed that in his weakened condition, he succumbed to the unusually low temperatures that Rawton has recently experienced.

She asked however, that people not be sad about Charlie's early death. The well-known degenerative change associated with that condition had not yet happened when he died.

'In this way,' she said, 'I will always be able to remember him as my beautiful boy. He was always a very cheerful lad, even though he spent so much time in hospital.' Wiping tears away, she added, 'Even when he was found, he didn't really look ill, despite the cold. He was looking up at the stars, smiling, like he was going home.'

Short Story First Prize

INDEX

Title	Author	Page
Advice to a stripling	Fran Baillie	10
A letter to my body	Emma Baker	36
An empty chair	Andy Allan	9
April day arrivals	Seth Crook	16
As days grow long	Marie-Thérèse Taylor	25
Beatha ùr	Deborah Moffatt	90
Beslotted	Neil Beaton	26
Black cat master	Neil Beaton	27
Blind faith	Swara Shukla	40
Blue angel on Union Street	Derek Brown	18
Charlotte	Colin Kerr	84
Chippies are always shut on Sundays	Paula Nicolson	57
Clay-cladded hearts	Sharon Boyle	54
Condorman (1981)	Jo Gilbert	32
Click	Meg Gannon	72
Daft and Dafter	Bert Thomson	82
Dreams	Emma Baker	34
Dreams	Leela Soma	74
Eulogy	Tom Gillespie	29
Figheachan	Peter Clive	86
Fish	Mary Wight	94
Glass drunk dry	Sharon Boyle	46
Going home	Montague Chambers	104
Guilt written	William Sutton	95
I do not like thee, Doctor Fell	Sharon Boyle	52
Intelligence test	Mary Nixon	20
I stand witness	Tom Gillespie	30
Kintsugi	Morag Anderson	28
Kirkintilloch Co-operative, 1960s	David McVey	23
Laundrette	Leela Soma	76
Listen	Aileen Paterson	60
Living the language	Elaine Webster	93

Title	Author	Page
Loch Thom revisited	A C Clarke	67
Looking out of a train window	Derek Crook	45
MacDougall's art studio and garage	Derek Crook	44
Marbhrann MhicCodruim dheireannaich	Sgàire Uallas	88
My mother's complaint when I moved north	Lynn Valentine	24
Now that I'm no longer dying	Jilly O'Brien	92
On the way to Skye	Ann MacKinnon	65
Orkney spring	Jane Lamb	39
Our child	Emma Baker	38
Out at sea	Ann MacKinnon	64
Poppies	A C Clarke	66
Rael warlds	Hamish Scott	56
Raisin Edzell Blues	Alun Robert	42
Rime	Jean Taylor	77
River	Meg Gannon	73
Safe place	Sue Proudlove	58
Scots Pine	Andy Allan	8
Scrapbook	Leela Soma	75
Snow in Venice	Sue Proudlove	59
Stanley	Jo Gilbert	33
Still not still	Greg Michaelson	62
Successors	David Betteridge	15
The attic	Sheila Millar	11
The great escape	Seth Crook	17
The man in the corner	Steve May	102
The permanent arrangement of Lilli Crabtree	Alan Gillespie	68
What good's a cowboy	Steve May	81
Wings	Aileen Paterson	61

Federation of Writers (Scotland)